Macramé Pattern Book

Includes Over 70 Knots and Small Repeat Patterns Plus Projects

Märchen Art Studio

Supervised by The Japan Macramé Association

St. Martin's Griffin
New York

Contents

No. 44   Diamond-shaped Patterns

Introduction

Tie one cord to another and make a knot: This is the basis of macramé. It is an action that we've all performed repeatedly in our daily lives without much thought. If you tie one cord around another once, you can make a simple knot. However, when you tie one knot after another, you can make a rope, or a large surface. Depending on the construction of the knot and the number of cords used, a limitless and infinite variety of patterns becomes possible.

Although its possibilities are endless, macramé requires little gear other than cord; you don't need any special tools. Because of the simplicity of this craft, macramé has long existed in many parts of the world. Many of the geometric patterns and plant and animal motifs that have been formed out of knots are folk designs common to several cultures.

With these knots, anyone can make embellishments such as buttons, trims and edgings, or even straps and handles that make lovely accents on fashion and home accessories. This book introduces you to a great variety of possibilities and invites you to makes some of our designs or create others of your own. To begin, flip through the pages of the book to find a pattern (or two, or three) that calls out to you.

This visual index will guide you to the directions for making each knot.

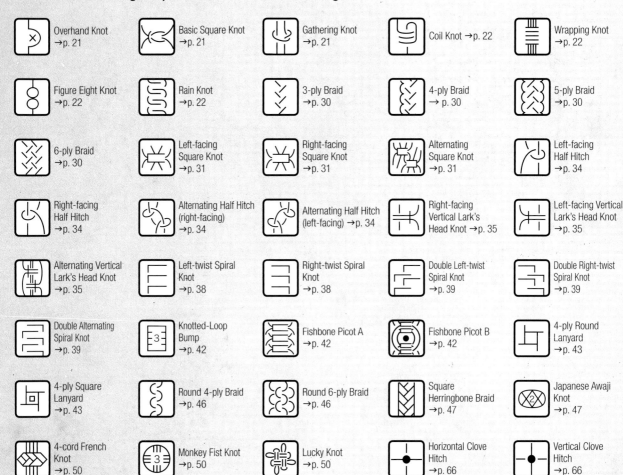

Overhand Knot →p. 21

Basic Square Knot →p. 21

Gathering Knot →p. 21

Coil Knot →p. 22

Wrapping Knot →p. 22

Figure Eight Knot →p. 22

Rain Knot →p. 22

3-ply Braid →p. 30

4-ply Braid → p. 30

5-ply Braid → p. 30

6-ply Braid →p. 30

Left-facing Square Knot →p. 31

Right-facing Square Knot →p. 31

Alternating Square Knot →p. 31

Left-facing Half Hitch →p. 34

Right-facing Half Hitch →p. 34

Alternating Half Hitch (right-facing) →p. 34

Alternating Half Hitch (left-facing) →p. 34

Right-facing Vertical Lark's Head Knot →p. 35

Left-facing Vertical Lark's Head Knot →p. 35

Alternating Vertical Lark's Head Knot →p. 35

Left-twist Spiral Knot →p. 38

Right-twist Spiral Knot →p. 38

Double Left-twist Spiral Knot →p. 39

Double Right-twist Spiral Knot →p. 39

Double Alternating Spiral Knot →p. 39

Knotted-Loop Bump →p. 42

Fishbone Picot A →p. 42

Fishbone Picot B →p. 42

4-ply Round Lanyard →p. 43

4-ply Square Lanyard →p. 43

Round 4-ply Braid →p. 46

Round 6-ply Braid →p. 46

Square Herringbone Braid →p. 47

Japanese Awaji Knot →p. 47

4-cord French Knot →p. 50

Monkey Fist Knot →p. 50

Lucky Knot →p. 50

Horizontal Clove Hitch →p. 66

Vertical Clove Hitch →p. 66

Diagonal Clove Hitch (right-facing) →p. 66

Diagonal Clove Hitch (left-facing) →p. 66

Reverse Horizontal Clove Hitch (right to left) →p. 66

Reverse Vertical Clove Hitch (left to right) →p. 66

How to Use this Book

• Chapter 01 provides an overview of the materials and basics you'll need to get started. Here you'll learn about cords, findings, and ways to plan, start, and finish your work.

• Chapter 02 is a guide to making knots and knotted patterns. You'll quickly see that macramé directions are given as diagrams with small bits of explanatory text. The knots and small repeating patterns are each denoted by a symbol (shown in the index above). The larger patterns are depicted with a graphic assemblage of these symbols: a diagram that shows the way the knots are placed, repeated, and connected. Once you examine the symbols and diagrams you'll see they are intuitive and easy to follow—much easier than reading lots of wordy instructions! You can try out any of these knots and patterns with any cord you have on hand: The amount required and the dimensions of the finished work will vary with the cord diameter.

• Chapter 03 offers a selection of projects and specifies cord types and colors. You may of course use whatever materials please you. Dimensions are given in both inches and centimeters, with cord lengths rounded up to the nearest whole number. Your knotting tension may be slightly different from that achieved by the samplemakers, so use the project dimensions as a guide, not a given. And feel free to make the items larger or smaller, either by using a different weight cord or by knotting more of it.

• This book was created in Japan; some of the materials pictured are not easily found in the U.S. Appropriate equivalents have been specified to the best of the publisher's ability, but the project dimensions and cord quantities may not be exactly the same as in the original—test your work before cutting all your cords. Specialty bead suppliers are a good source of fine (thin) cords.

Macramé
Pattern
Book

Prologue

**A fascinating history,
a world of tradition**

What Is Macramé?

When you hear the term macramé, what image springs to mind? A mesh-patterned rustic twine bag? A patterned belt knotted out of leather or string? An accessory of some sort woven out of thin cord and metal or stone beads? Or perhaps a slightly retro bowl cover or owl ornament? Some people may know these items but never have heard the word macramé.

The term macramé refers broadly to the craft of knotting cords together decoratively to make objects. Any string, thread, or cord that can be tied will work. Typically, hemp, jute, leather, silk, or cotton cords are used, but knitting yarn, kite string, embroidery thread, rayon or other synthetic cords—and really any type of cord that you may have lying around—can be used too.

Macramé has been used in many different ways. In addition to its use for the typical bags and belts mentioned above, it has a long history as a trim (often including a fringe) for the edges of shawls and stoles, linens and curtains; macramé tassels are classic and can be magnificent. Once we call attention to the different iterations of macramé, most people realize they have some familiarity with the craft.

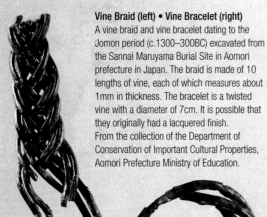

Vine Braid (left) • Vine Bracelet (right)
A vine braid and vine bracelet dating to the Jomon period (c.1300–300BC) excavated from the Sannai Maruyama Burial Site in Aomori prefecture in Japan. The braid is made of 10 lengths of vine, each of which measures about 1mm in thickness. The bracelet is a twisted vine with a diameter of 7cm. It is possible that they originally had a lacquered finish.
From the collection of the Department of Conservation of Important Cultural Properties, Aomori Prefecture Ministry of Education.

Shutora
The word Shutora comes from the Sanskrit word sutra, which refers to sacred religious texts. The shutora on the right is said to represent the sacred texts of Buddhism. Such braided cords came to Japan with Buddhism, and even today when Buddhist priests wear a type of robe called a Shichijogesa (Striped Buddhist Priest's Stole), they drape a similar cord over their shoulders. Those used today are long, thickly braided silk cords, while this example on the right is much smaller, about the size of a strap.

The History of Macramé

The simple act of braiding and tying cord into something useful probably dates back to the time when humans first started using tools. In Aomori prefecture in Japan, a braided plant vine and bracelet (below left) were excavated from the Sannai Maruyama Burial Site, the remains of a settlement dating to the Jomon period (c.1300–300BC).

The word Jomon itself actually refers to a rope pattern that was impressed onto the surface of the characteristic ceramics of the period. It is thought that the rope pattern is linked to a belief among the Jomon people that knots contained a magical power that could bring about longevity and fertility. In other words, knots served a type of protective charm or talisman.

The tradition of knotting is not limited to Japan. Because knotting is such a simple handcraft, techniques and interpretations evolved all over the world and were cultivated within the customs and culture of every region. Consider: We learned to tie a square knot and braid a lanyard as children; this knowledge is useful to us in our daily lives, and has been passed through generations as part of our day-to-day knowledge, literally becoming the "thread of life." It is very difficult, therefore, for us to know the precise origins of knotting itself.

It is also hard to be clear about the development of macramé for decorative materials in the modern world. The word macramé itself is believed to come from an Arabic word meaning "knotting crossways" or "ornamental fringe." Knotting techniques that were originally used to finish off the edges of textiles and cloth gradually took on a more decorative quality, and it is believed that the craft evolved in Eastern Europe, Western Asia, the Middle East, and Northern Africa. During the Middle Ages, techniques that were developed in the Islamic world, which was the most

Antique cloths from Romania (left) and Hungary (right)
When these cloths were made, about 100 years ago, production of handmade textiles was very labor-intensive, with many women growing and spinning their own fibers, weaving the spun threads into cloth, and then decorating the cloth with embroidery. In Romania and Hungary, women traditionally decorated the edges of towels, shawls, and similar textiles with fine lacelike macramé fringes as well.

Buddhist Treasure Mesh bags
In the Japanese tea ceremony not only the vessels but also the baskets and bags that they were wrapped and stored in were appreciated as objects of admiration. Macramé pieces such as this beautifully patterned Buddhist Treasure Mesh bag have long been used to wrap tea bowls and tea caddies. Each bag or pouch was unique as its shape and color were chosen to match the vessel it contained.

advanced cultural realm of the time, were transmitted to Italy as trade expanded to Asia and Europe. Knotting techniques also seem to have developed independently in various regions in Europe.

In Italy, artisans in the city of Genoa developed the greatest variety of macramé types in the world. Even today, macramé is more popular in Genoa than in any other city. In the sixteenth and seventeenth centuries, in Europe, macramé enjoyed tremendous popularity as a decorative detail in women's clothes. In Victorian Britain in the nineteenth century, after the Queen taught macramé to the ladies of the Court, it became extremely popular there, and many ladies took great pleasure from braiding delicate macramé decorations out of fine cords and threads.

During Europe's colonial period, when there was a great movement of people and things, macramé spread to new regions—from Spain to Mexico, from France to Quebec in Canada, from Genoa to North and South America. The word macramé was adopted from Arabic into French, and from French into English and is now understood all over the world.

Macramé as we know it today was first enjoyed in Japan during the Meiji period (1868–1912), when Japan was adopting many aspects of European culture. Since then, at the start of the Showa period (1926–89), then after World War II, and then again in the 1980s, there have been several periods when macramé has enjoyed great popularity.

Among the patterns in this book—both classic and idiosyncratic—some may appear so complicated at first glance that you'll find it hard to guess how they were made. But, actually, once you understand the basics of two macramé knots—the Square Knot (on p. 31) and the Clove Hitch (also known as the Double Half Hitch, on p. 66), you will see how these have been adapted and configured in many diverse ways to create the patterns in this book. Whatever anyone may say, because the foundation of macramé is the simple technique of tying a knot with cord, once you master the technique, all that remains is to repeat the process in a creative way. When you experience the moment of joy when a pattern emerges from your hands, you will begin to want to knot all sorts of things.

In this book it is possible to introduce only a small sampling of the many variations of macramé knotting that exist. From these, we have carefully selected some basic techniques that we believe are important to master, some standard patterns that are widely used, and some patterns that have broad applications and can be easily adapted to create functional objects. When we consider the number of hands that these patterns have passed through over many generations, each pattern seems like a tiny time capsule.

Macramé, a handcraft that has been passed down through the generations and brightened up people's daily life all over the world, can be found today in craft objects full of warmth and simplicity and in fashion and home accessories, where it may be chic or artisanal (or both!) according to your eye. We have gathered here a number of macramé items from different parts of the world. Similar knotting patterns are in Chapter 02 of this book.

Madagascar: Sisal Bags

Madagascar is an island nation in the Indian Ocean just off the east coast of continental Africa. A special kind of rope made from sisal fiber (from a local agave plant) is used in the manufacture of intricately knotted macramé bags, which are exported to far away countries.

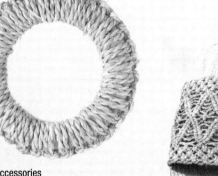

Turkey: Protective Charm

In Turkey, a Narzar Boncugu, a protective amulet in the form of an eye made of blue glass, is believed to have the power to ward off the evil eye and keep bad luck at bay. If you visit a Turkish souvenir shop, you will see many different items, such as key chains and accessories, decorated with this talisman. At left is a simple example, mounted on a chunky hemp tassel made using macramé techniques.

Sado Island, Japan: Pot Trivet

This is a pot trivet made by a farming family on Sado Island, Japan. This household object, tightly knotted from rice straw, reflects the wisdom of farmers who let nothing go to waste from their harvests.

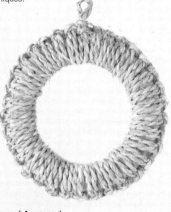

Macramé Accessories

If you visit a shop that specializes in ethnic goods, you will often see macramé accessories such as bracelets, anklets, and necklaces. They come from such countries as Mexico, Peru in South America, or Indonesia and other counties in Southeast Asia. Each region has different patterns and knotting techniques, and they are made using a variety of materials, including hemp, waxed cord, leather, and wool.

Bangladesh: Jute Sandals

Jute is a natural fiber that is a staple material in Bangladesh, where women use it to make various handmade fair-trade products, such as these sandals, as a means of earning an income.

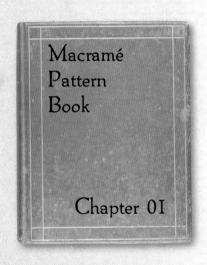

Macramé
Pattern
Book

Chapter 01

Getting Started in Macramé

Make yourself comfortable
We recommend attaching the macramé cords to a knotting board (→p. 15) so you can maintain an even tension in your work. Sitting with the board upright in your lap and leaning against a table is the easiest and most comfortable way to do macramé work.

Any Type of Cord Can Be Used

In macramé, you can use any type of cord that can be knotted. Whether you prefer the natural look of hemp, the cool appearance of leather, the intricacy that can be achieved with finer types of cord, the bright colors of perle cotton for friendship bracelets, or traditional macramé cords, you can select the type and the thickness you need, depending on what you want to make. The selection of the material is one of the joys of macramé.

However, even though any of these materials can be used in macramé, a supple cord that has some elasticity is easiest for beginners to knot into a neat form.

Hemp and Jute

For macramé, a commonly used fiber is hemp, a fast-crowing plant that thrives without the use of pesticides and so is known for its pure, organic qualities. Hemp cords have a very natural appearance and are manufactured in different colors and thicknesses, from the fine cords used for accessories and the thicker cords used to make bags and mats. Jute, a similar rustic fiber, is another common choice. Both hemp and jute twine are readily available, but you may find the best selection of colors and fine weights online and in specialty bead stores. In this book, many samples are made from Jute Ramie, a softer and more polished blended fiber cord for which linen cord could be a good substitute (as could pure jute). There can be issues with both hemp and jute; for example, if the cords are not of handcraft quality, the fibers will fray easily and can have a strong smell. Of course, we recommend using handicraft quality cords. Also, hemp and other similar fibers shrink when wet, so be careful when they get dirty to only wipe them with a cloth. If you have to wash them, only do so by hand.

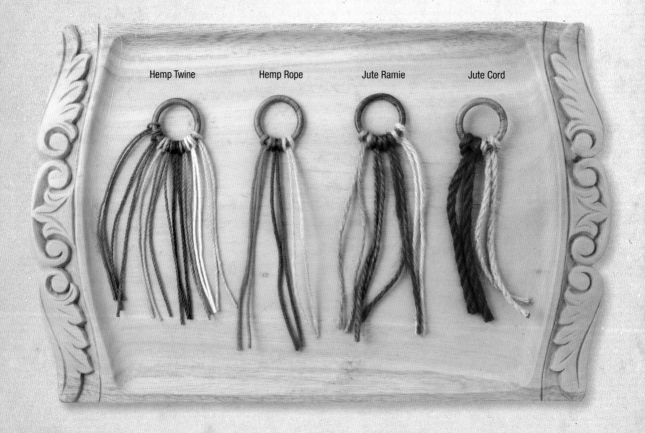

Hemp Twine   Hemp Rope   Jute Ramie   Jute Cord

Leather

For accessories like belts and bags, leather is a great choice. There are many variations and textures to choose from, including flat lace, round cords, and suede, each of which comes in many hues. When leather gets wet, the color bleeds and can stain other objects, so care should be taken when choosing colored leather. It should also be stored away from direct sunlight.

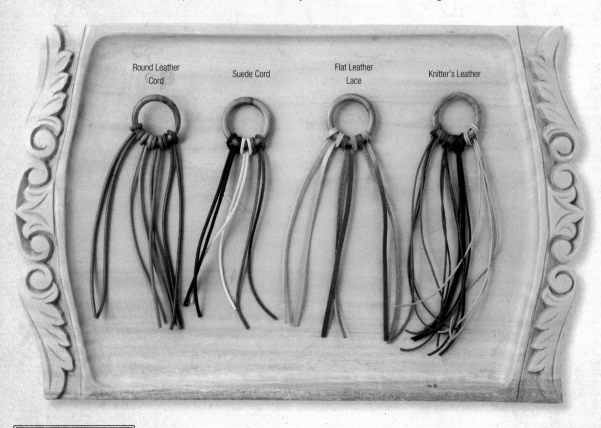

Round Leather Cord

Suede Cord

Flat Leather Lace

Knitter's Leather

Fashion Cords

Cotton Cord
We like a fine cotton cord with a polished surface that has a nice sheen.

Braided Cord
This is often labeled "macramé cord"; made of polyester, it has a sheen.

Waxed Cord
This polyester cord has been treated with a wax finish. As it is knotted, the strands fit snuggly together, creating very neat knots.

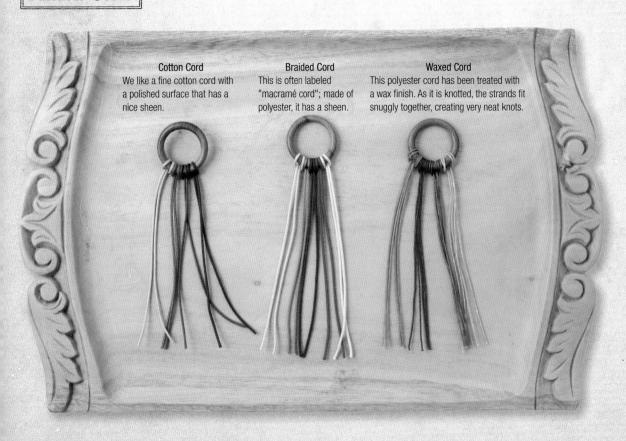

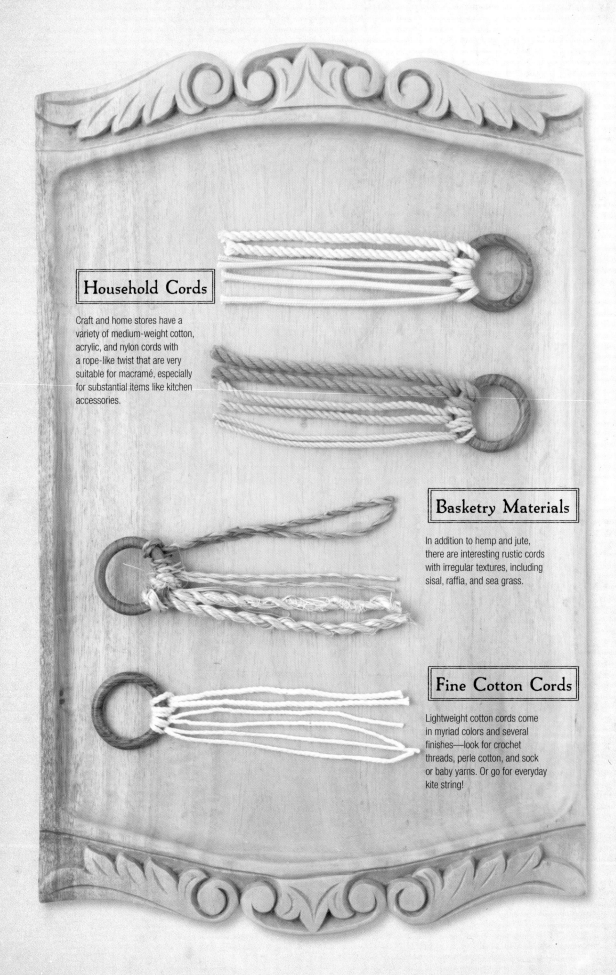

Household Cords

Craft and home stores have a variety of medium-weight cotton, acrylic, and nylon cords with a rope-like twist that are very suitable for macramé, especially for substantial items like kitchen accessories.

Basketry Materials

In addition to hemp and jute, there are interesting rustic cords with irregular textures, including sisal, raffia, and sea grass.

Fine Cotton Cords

Lightweight cotton cords come in myriad colors and several finishes—look for crochet threads, perle cotton, and sock or baby yarns. Or go for everyday kite string!

Lesson
02

Essential Tools • Useful Tools

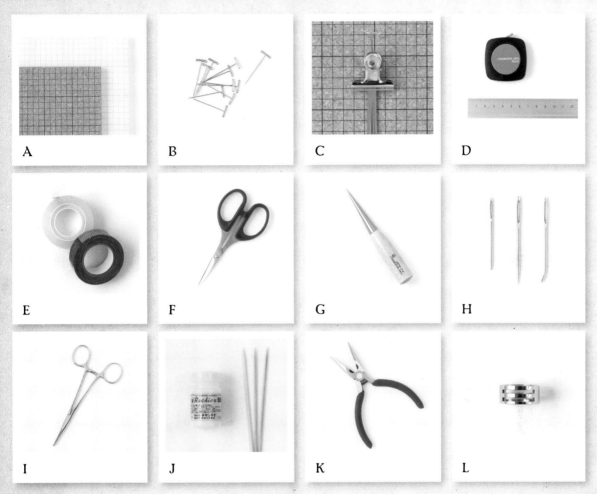

A

B

C

D

E

F

G

H

I

J

K

L

A. Knotting Board
A pinnable board to which you attach the cords. Specialist boards have a grid printed on them, which can serve as a guide to pattern spacing.

B. Macramé Pins
These are used to attach the cords to the board. T-pins and push pins work fine.

C. Binder Clip
When cords are too thick to be pinned to the board, they can be gripped by a clip that can be pinned instead.

D. Measuring Tape. Ruler
Used to measure the length of cords and the dimensions of pattern surfaces. Depending on its size, a ruler can also be used as a spacer to establish row height when knotting mesh patterns.

E. Adhesive Tapes
If you are not using a knotting board, you can tape the ends of the cords to your desk. In addition, tape can be wrapped around the cord ends to stop them from fraying. Also, if you need to give your hands a rest, you can use tape to hold your work in place. If you are concerned the tape might impair the surface of the material you are using, use easily removable painter's blue tape.

F. Scissors
It is best to use specialty craft scissors.

G. Awl
Poke the tip of an awl between cords to help tighten or loosen the knots.

H. Large-eye Sewing Needle
Tapestry and yarn needles are needed to weave cord ends into the back of the work when you are finished knotting.

I. Forceps
Can be used to pull a cord through a space between or within a knot. Not necessary but very useful.

J. Glue and Bamboo Skewers
Strong craft glue can be used to secure final knots and prevent fraying. Use bamboo skewers or another tool with a narrow tip to apply the glue neatly and protect your fingers.

K. Pliers
Needed to attach various findings and clasps. This can be finicky work; small needle-nose pliers are most useful.

L. Small Clamp
Use a ring clamp or another "third hand" to hold part of the work steady when you are attaching clasps or other findings.

Charms, Beads, and Findings Add to the Fun

Various decorative embellishments such as beads and charms can be incorporated into macramé items. As you decide the look you want for your design, consider the materials and style of the embellishments. Findings such as clasps and rings are often required for jewelry or to affix straps. Choose these items thoughtfully to give your macramé panache.

Charms

Small charms, pendants, and buttons can be key design components for accessories such as necklaces, tassels, and key rings. They come in a variety of materials and finishes. A charm can also be a protective talisman and there are many lucky charm motifs to choose among—from all around the world. Assemble a collection of these appealing embellishments.

Beads

Beads are a lovely complement to macramé and can be used in a variety of ways. Place them between knots, at the tip of fringe, or incorporate them into an allover pattern as part of the detailing. There is a rich variety available—stone, glass, wood, bone, clay, and metal—in many forms and with different surface patterns. Make sure your cord will fit through any beads you consider.

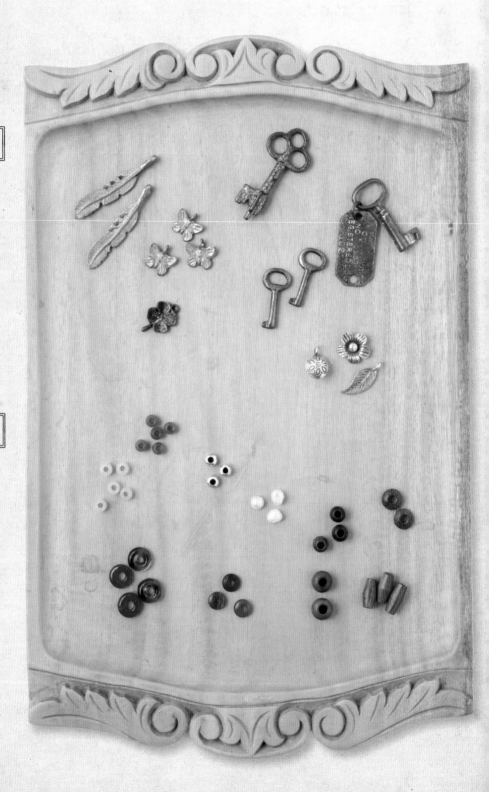

Jewelry Clasps

The metal closures designed
for necklaces and bracelets
come in a variety of styles, but
there are many are items, such
as bars; rings, shank buttons,
and toggle buttons that can
also be used effectively. The
trick is to select pieces that go
well with the style of the cords
and knotting used.

Metal Hardware

Often you'll want to attach
a macramé strap or similar
piece to another item, say a
cloth bag or a camera. Metal
trigger hooks, rings, and
various other bits of hardware
play an aesthetic as well as
functional role when this is the
case. Choose hardware that is
in scale for your project.

Wood Parts

Small wooden rings have
many uses, such as a fob for
a key chain, to connect a strap
to a bag, or as a belt buckle.
We like the warm, folky look of
wood mixed with macramé.

How to Start a Macramé Project

The way you begin a macramé project depends on the type of object you choose to make: a narrow piece such as a necklace, which we'll call a sennit, or a wider fabric such as a mat, which we'll call a panel, and also on options such as loop closures or fringe. Once you decide, refer to this chart to get started: in each box, choose A or B as it applies to you and then follow the arrow to the next step.
<Text in Boxes; Left to right, top row)>

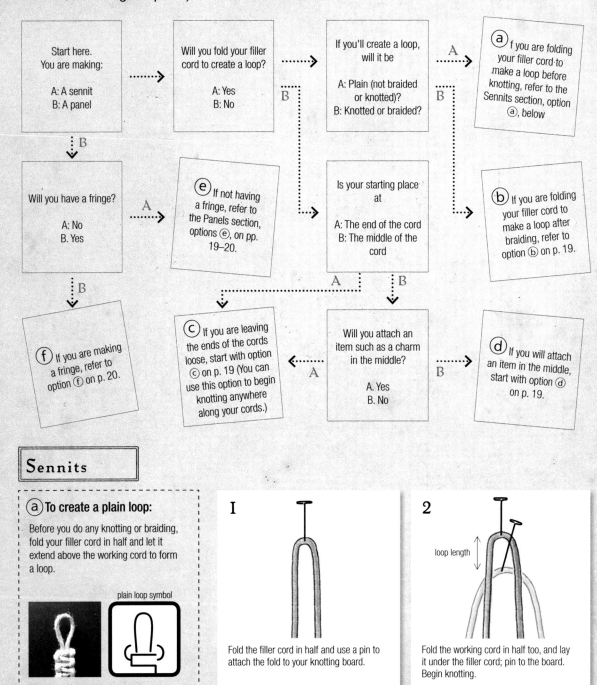

Start here.
You are making:

A: A sennit
B: A panel

Will you fold your filler cord to create a loop?

A: Yes
B: No

If you'll create a loop, will it be

A: Plain (not braided or knotted)?
B: Knotted or braided?

(a) f you are folding your filler cord to make a loop before knotting, refer to the Sennits section, option (a), below

Will you have a fringe?

A: No
B. Yes

(e) If not having a fringe, refer to the Panels section, options (e), on pp. 19–20.

Is your starting place at

A: The end of the cord
B: The middle of the cord

(b) If you are folding your filler cord to make a loop after braiding, refer to option (b) on p. 19.

(f) If you are making a fringe, refer to option (f) on p. 20.

(c) If you are leaving the ends of the cords loose, start with option (c) on p. 19 (You can use this option to begin knotting anywhere along your cords.)

Will you attach an item such as a charm in the middle?

A. Yes
B. No

(d) If you will attach an item in the middle, start with option (d) on p. 19.

Sennits

(a) To create a plain loop:

Before you do any knotting or braiding, fold your filler cord in half and let it extend above the working cord to form a loop.

plain loop symbol

1

Fold the filler cord in half and use a pin to attach the fold to your knotting board.

2

loop length

Fold the working cord in half too, and lay it under the filler cord; pin to the board. Begin knotting.

(b) To create a knotted or braided loop

If the sennit you are making has 2 or more filler cords, you may knot or braid a loop at the starting end.

braided loop symbol

I

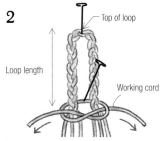

Pin
Temporary knot
Start knotting
2x loop length
Top of loop

Hold the filler cords together. Loosely tie an overhand knot (→p. 21) a short distance from their midpoint and pin to your board. Braid or knot the cords for twice the length desired for your loop.

2

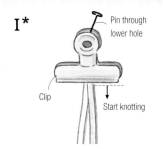

Top of loop
Loop length
Working cord

Untie the temporary knot; fold the braided section in half and pin the fold to the board. Position the working cord around the braided loop; pin to the board. Begin knotting.

(c) To start with the ends left loose

Use this technique if you want to begin your sennit without creating a loop—you may begin knotting near 1 end or anywhere along the filler cord you like.

loose ends symbol

I

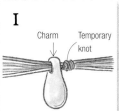

Start knotting
Temporary knot

Hold the filler cords together. Loosely tie an overhand knot (→p. 21) where you wish to begin knotting; pin to your board. Begin knotting.

I*

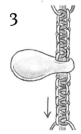

Pin through lower hole
Clip
Start knotting

When using leather cord, secure the filler cords with a small binder clip and pin the clip to your board.

(d) To start by attaching a charm in the middle

Start this way if you wish to attach a charm or pendant at the middle of your sennit.

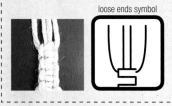
central charm symbol

I

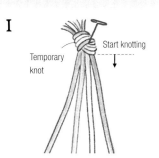

Charm   Temporary knot

Hold the filler cords together. Loosely tie an overhand knot (→p. 21) at the midpoint, where you wish to position the charm. Insert the filler cord ends through the charm; slide the charm to the knot.

2

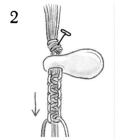

Place the work on your board with the knot above the charm; pin the knot to the board. Begin knotting below the charm.

3

When you finish knotting the cords below the charm, unpin the work and untie the knot. Return the work to the board with the knotted section above the charm, and knot the remaining section.

Panels

(e) To set up a panel without fringe (Version A)

Here is the most basic way to attach working cords to an anchor cord.

attach w/loop up symbol

I

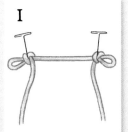

Tie an overhand knot (→p. 21) at each end of the anchor cord; stretch the cord and pin it to your board through the knots.

I*

If you are making a tubular piece (such as a bag), stretch the anchor cord around the knotting board and, leaving both ends long enough to become working cords, tie it together at 1 edge of the board.

2

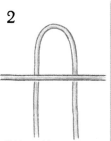

Fold a working cord in half and slide it under the anchor cord with the loop pointing up (continued on p. 20).

3

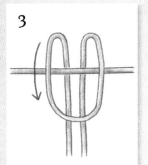

Fold the loop of the working cord down over the anchor cord.

4

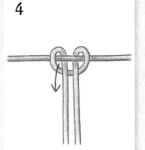

Pull both ends of the working cord all the way through the loop, tightening the loop against the anchor cord.

4*-a

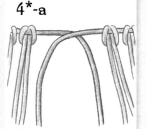

Add more working cords in the same way. If you are making a tubular piece, add cords all around, then untie the anchor cord and overlap it, allowing the ends to dangle.

4*-b

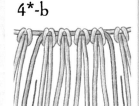

Add more working cords over the doubled section of anchor cord, counting the total you need minus 2. The dangling ends of the anchor cords now count as the final 2 working cords.

ⓔ **To set up a panel without fringe (Version B)**

This technique is essentially the same as Version A, but the initial position of the working cord is inverted, so the loop of the finished knot faces you. Begin with step 1 of Version A.

attach w/loop down symbol

2

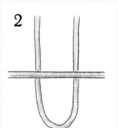

Fold a working cord in half and slide it under the anchor chord with the loop pointing down.

3

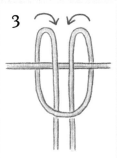

Pull both ends of the working cord down through the loop.

4

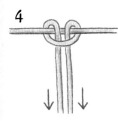

Pull the ends of the working cord to tighten the loop against the anchor cord.

ⓔ **To set up a panel without fringe (Version C)**

Use this variation of Version A to create a wider knot at the top of each working cord. Begin with step 1 of Version A.

attach w/wide knot symbol

2

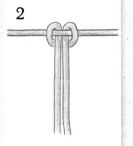

Tie a working cord to the anchor cord following steps 2–4 of Version A.

3

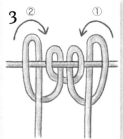

Follow this diagram to wrap each end of the working cord around the anchor cord again, inserting each through the new loop it forms.

4

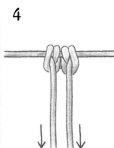

Pull the ends of the working cord to tighten the new loops against the anchor cord.

ⓕ **To set up a panel with fringe**

Use this technique to attach working cords so they extend on both sides of the anchor cord, allowing you to knot one side into a fabric and create a fringe with the other side.

attach w/fringe symbol

1

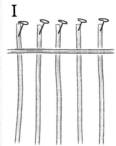

Follow ⓔ step 1 on page 19 to set up the anchor cord. Pin working cords under it as shown here, letting them extend above as needed for your desired fringe.

2

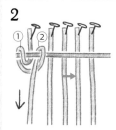

Loop a working cord around the anchor cord twice following the path shown here (making a Horizontal Clove Hitch →p. 66).

3

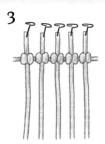

Pull the cord ends to tighten the knot. Repeat for the remaining working cords. Remove the pins when finished.

Techniques for Knotting Cord Ends

Here is an assortment of basic knots that can be used to secure or tie the ends of the cords—either temporarily or permanently. Most are not used to create macramé patterns, but they are very handy and important to master.

Overhand Knot

Used to reinforce other knots and to tie together multiple strands. The more strands that are tied together, the larger the knot.

overhand knot symbol

I

Pass the cord end around itself and through the loop it forms, as indicated by the arrow.

2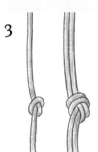

Pull the end of the cord to tightly close the knot.

3

Hold multiple strands of cord together to tie in the same way.

Square Knot

A basic knot that is also used to create many macramé patterns.

square knot symbol

I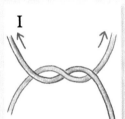

Pass the top (brown) cord over, under, and then over the bottom (red) cord as shown.

2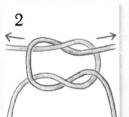

Now cross the 2 cords as shown by the arrows, passing the end of each through the loop formed by the other.

3

Pull both ends of both cords to tighten the knot.

Gathering Knot

A simple way to tie 3 or more cords together. Since only 1 cord does the tying, the knot is always small, regardless of the number of cords secured.

gathering knot symbol

I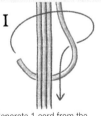

Separate 1 cord from the group and pass its end around the others and itself, and then through the loop it forms, as indicated by the arrow.

2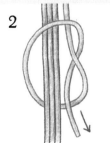

Pull the end of the tying cord to tightly close the knot.

3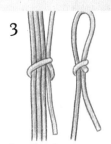

Done. If you loop a single cord and tie it this way (as on the right), a slipknot forms.

Coil Knot

Use this technique to make a longer knot on a single cord. The length of the knot will vary depending on the number of times you wind the cord.

coil knot symbol

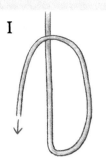

1 Pass the end of the cord up and over itself so that it forms a loop as shown.

2 Wind the end of the cord 3 times (or more) around the left side of the loop.

3 To tighten the knot, hold 1 end of the cord in each hand and gently pull up the end that extends above the coil.

Wrapping Knot

Use this technique when you'd like a substantial binding around a group of cords. Turn the work around as you wrap to make sure the binding is neat and without gaps.

wrapping knot symbol

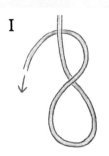

1 Fold a long working cord (in red on the diagram) and lay it against the filler cords as shown. Wrap end B around and around, starting at the top and ending ⅝"/0.5 cm above the folded loop (C).

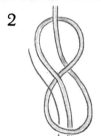

2 Pass end B of the wrapping cord through loop C.

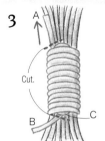

3 Pull up cord end A to slide loop C inside the wrapped binding. Cut off ends A and B close to the binding.

Figure Eight Knot

A simple, decorative knot that looks especially nice tied in a thick cord or group of thin cords handled as one.

figure eight knot symbol

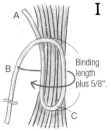

1 Loop the end of the cord around to form a figure eight as shown.

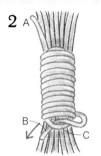

2 Follow the path of the arrow to pass the end of the cord through the lower loop.

3 Pull the cord above and below the knot, adjusting the shape as you close the knot.

Rain Knot

A knot made with 2 cords. If tied one after another, this knot will form a chain with an even bumpy texture.

rain knot symbol

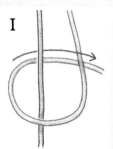

1 Loosely tie the right (red) cord over the left cord as shown.

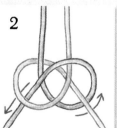

2 Follow the path of the arrows to loosely pass the left cord behind and then forward over the right cord, inserting it through the loop made in step 1.

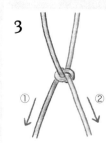

3 Hold the knot between the fingers of 1 hand and, with the other hand, pull first the left cord and then the right cord to tighten it.

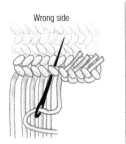

Tidying up the loose end of a filler cord or anchor cord

When you need to hide the end of a filler cord or an anchor cord, use a yarn needle or large tapestry needle to pass the cord through the knots on the wrong side of the work.

Wrong side

Tidying up the loose end of a working cord

Wrong side

Similarly, when you need to hide the ends of working cords, use a yarn needle or large tapestry needle to pass each cord through the knots on the wrong side.

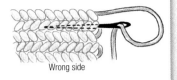

Lesson
06

7 Tips for Neat Knotting

For macramé to be successful, all the knots must be consistent and aligned appropriately for the design. This may seem a little difficult at first, but there are some helpful tricks for controlling the cords; if you use them, it is surprisingly easy to keep your knotting even and smooth.

Tip-1   Bundle the Cords to Prevent Tangling

If you wrap and tie each cord into a small bundle before you begin to work, it will be much easier to manipulate your knotting and keep the cords from tangling. If the cords are long, wrap them as shown and unspool them as you work; short cords can be wrapped and secured with a rubber band. In the case of working cords, the smaller the bundles, the easier it is to pass them through loops.

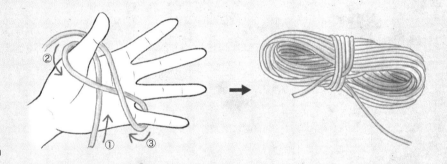

Tip-2   Work with a Little More Cord than You Need

The length of cord required for a project will differ depending on the type of knots used, the arrangement of the knots and the tightness, or tension, of your work. This chart can be used as a reference to estimate the length of cord necessary for certain types of knots. Usually, project instructions will tell you how much cord you need, but the amount actually used can vary with the type of cord and your tension. So when you cut your cords, it's safer to give yourself a little extra length.

Type of Knot	Estimated Cord Length	Type of Knot	Estimated Cord Length
Square Knot	5–6 times the length of the finished piece	Alternating Square or Lark's Head Knots	4–5 times the length of the finished piece
Spiral Knot	5–6 times the length of the finished piece	Buddhist Treasure Mesh (1 knot, ¾"/2cm intervals)	2–2½ times the length of the finished piece
Clove Hitch	6–7 times the length of the finished piece	Wrapping Knot	2–2½ times the length of the finished knot
Lark's Head Knot	6–7 times the length of the finished piece	Awaji Knot	2½–3 times the diameter of the finished knot

23

Tip-3　Keep Your Tension Even

The strength with which you tighten the knots affects the consistency of their size. Practice until you find a rhythm and see that your knots are consistent, lying flat (not twisted), and evenly spaced. If you notice the work looking loose, pull firmly on the anchor cord or filler cord to tighten the spacing.

Tip-4　Begin with a Sample Swatch

To calculate more precisely how much cord you will need for a piece, we recommend you do some test knotting—a sample swatch—with the actual cord you will be using before you start.

For sennits, make a swatch 2–4"/5–10cm long, and for panels, make a swatch about 2–4"/5–10cm square. Cut a measured length of each cord before you begin, and when done, measure the length remaining to see how much you actually used. Then use this figure to calculate the total length of cord you will need to make the complete piece.

Tip-5　Mark Your Cord Ends

To avoid confusion, particularly when you are creating a pattern with multiple cords of the same color, attach a label of some sort to the end of each cord so you can identify it. Choose a labeling material that is suitable for the fiber, won't get in the way, and won't fall off, for instance: colored stickers or bits of tape on which you write numbers or letters.

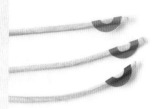

Tip-6　Tape Cord Ends for Easier Threading

When you have to pass 2 cords through a bead or similar object, first wrap their ends together with a bit of tape. If you then want to pass a third or fourth cord through the same bead, insert those cords between the first 2 (as in the far right drawing). You will be able to pull all the strands smoothly through from the other side of the bead.

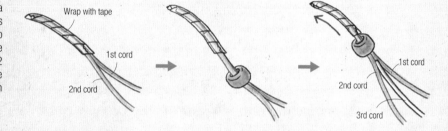

Wrap with tape

1st cord

2nd cord

1st cord

2nd cord

3rd cord

Tip-7　Use a Grid to Keep Patterns Even

One beauty of macramé is the variety of pattern that can be created simply by tying knots in specific arrangements. To ensure that the position of the knots in your chosen pattern is correct, it helps to check them as you work; this is especially true for mesh patterns.

As you can see in photo 1, one of the easiest methods for keeping a pattern even is to scale it to the grid on the knotting board. Secure the work to the board by pinning through each knot, and tie subsequent knots at intervals that match the grid.

Another method for ensuring consistency is to use a bar (such as a ruler) as a spacer between horizontal rows, as in photo 2; this is handy if you do

not have a knotting board. First analyze the way your knot will be formed so you can slide the bar consistently between the cords, and then tie the cords snugly against it.

If you are making a tubular piece, like a bag, the cords from the front and back layers can easily become tangled. To prevent this, slide a sheet of graph paper between them before you position your work on the board; then pin through all layers, as in photo 3. Tie the knots on the top layer, unpin, turn the entire work over so the bottom layer is on top, re-pin, and proceed.

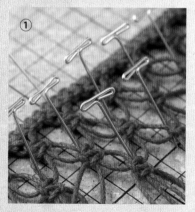

①

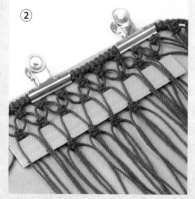

②

③

Lesson
07

Macramé Troubleshooting Q&A

No matter how well prepared you are when you start your knotting, you may find yourself getting stuck from time to time. The following are some methods for preventing and dealing with tricky situations.

Question-1 — Why do my macramé pins keep coming out?

A. There is a trick to pinning macramé knots to the board. Make sure the pin is leaning in the opposite direction from which you will be pulling the working cord. If it is leaning in the same direction, it is likely you'll pull it out.

Pinning through the cord itself can cause fraying, so either pin through a knot (between the cords) or, if you have to pin down the end of the cord, tie a loop and pin through it.

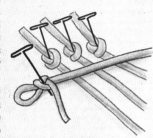

Question-2 — I found a mistake. What should I do?

A. This happens to everyone at some point. All you can do is undo all the knotting until you get back to the mistake, correct it, and then redo the portion you took out. If you find you must undo your knots, work carefully, using pins to keep the piece taut and an awl to gently tease the knots apart.

To avoid having to go back and correct earlier mistakes, keep checking your work as you go along.

Question-3 — What do I do if I run out of cord in the middle of my work?

A. There are a few ways to add more cord in order to fix this problem, each designed to remedy to a different situation, as explained below and on p. 26. No matter which you use, be sure to leave long tails of cord at the join for threading into a large needle and weaving into the wrong side of your work when you're finished.

❦ If you run out of the right and the left working cords on a sennit

Use this technique to add a new working cord to each edge of your work (shown with Square Knots →p. 31).

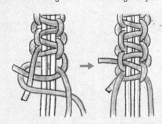

(Front of work)
Fold the new working cord in half and loop it around the sennit, feeding the original working cords through as shown. Continue.

(Back of work)
When the piece is completely knotted, hide the ends of the original working cords by inserting them into the knots on the wrong side (→p. 23).

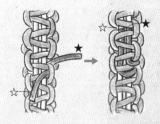

❦ If you run out of working cord on one edge of a sennit

Use this technique to a new working cord to just 1 edge of a your work (shown with Square Knots →p. 31).

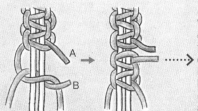

(Front of work)
Tie the end of the original cord to the end of the new cord using a Square Knot. Tie a couple more knots, then pull the ends A and B together tightly so that you don't leave any gaps.

(Back of work)
When the piece is completely knotted, hide the ends of the original cord and new cord by inserting them into the knots on the wrong side (→p. 23). To keep the surface even, turn 1 end up and the other down.

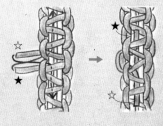

🌿 If you run out of 2 filler cords on a sennit (Version A)

This method of adding new filler cords makes a strong connection and leaves only 2 loose ends to weave into your finished work (shown with Square Knots →p. 31).

(Front of work)
Fold the ends of the original filler cords up, toward the back of the sennit. Fold the new filler cord in half and lay it into the upturned cord ends as shown. Continue knotting, leaving the ends of the original filler cords sticking out.

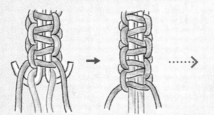

(Back of work)
When the piece is completely knotted, thread the ends of the original cords up, hiding them inside the work.

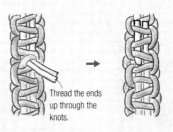

Thread the ends up through the knots.

🌿 If you run out of 2 filler cords on a sennit (Version B)

This easy method of adding new filler cords is not as strong as the previous one.

(Front of work)
Before the old filler cords run out, overlap them with the new filler cord ends. Continue knotting, taking care not to pull out the new filler cords.

(Front of work)
The ends of the cords are already hidden inside the knots, so there is no need to weave them in.

🌿 If you run out of 1 filler cord and 1 working cord on a sennit

You can use a single new cord to replace 1 filler cord and 1 working cord at the same time (shown with Square Knots →p. 31).

(Front of work)
Fold the new cord in half and secure it in the loop of the next knot you tie as shown. Continue knotting, using 1 strand of the new cord for filler, the other for knotting.

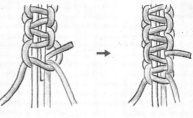

(Back of work)
When the knotting is complete, insert the ends of the original cords under the knots on the wrong side.

🌿 If you run out of a working cord on a panel

Whether you've run out of cord or wish to change colors, it's easy to add a new working cord midway through your work.

(Front of work)
Simply tie the next knot in sequence with a new length of cord, leaving a tail (shown with Clove Hitches, →p. 66).

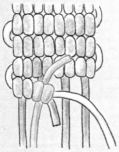

(Back of work)
When the knotting is complete, insert the ends of the original cords under the knots on the wrong side.

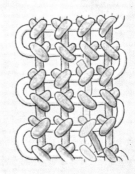

🌿 If you run out of an anchor cord on a panel

It's also easy to add an anchor cord in the middle of your work.

(Front of work)
Simply hold a new length of cord where you need it and tie the next knot in the sequence over it (shown with Clove Hitches →p. 66).

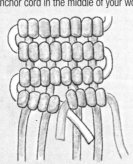

(Back of work)
When the piece is completely knotted, cross the ends of the original cords to close any gap and insert each under the knots on the wrong side.

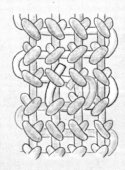

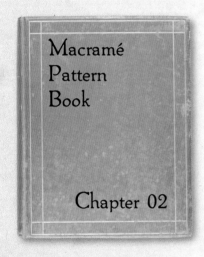

Macramé
Pattern
Book

Chapter 02

Macramé Patterns

How to Read a Knotting Diagram for a Macramé Panel

In Chapter 2, we introduce basic knots and show how to create 70 different patterns with them: 22 Sennit Patterns (for narrow pieces such as necklaces) and 48 Panel Patterns (for wider work such as mats), plus a few buttons and tassels. The knotting patterns for panels are shown in schematic drawings like this. Here's how to follow one:

• Each symbol corresponds to a specific knot; in this chapter, the key to the directions for that knot is next to the diagram.

• Generally, the knotting is worked in horizontal rows. The heavier top line represents the anchor cord; the dots on it represent the knots that tie the working cords to the anchor cord.

• Always begin by attaching the specified number of working cords to the anchor cord. Then read down to follow the diagram row by row.

• The numbers on the right are the row numbers. In addition, the area shaded in pink indicates the number of rows needed to complete a design unit (often called a repeat) used in a particular pattern. You may repeat this design unit until your work is the length you desire, but usually you'll want to finish knotting with the bottom row of a repeat so the pattern looks complete.

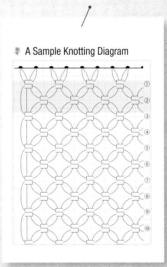

A Sample Knotting Diagram

Sennit Patterns
Basic Knots, Braids, and Bands

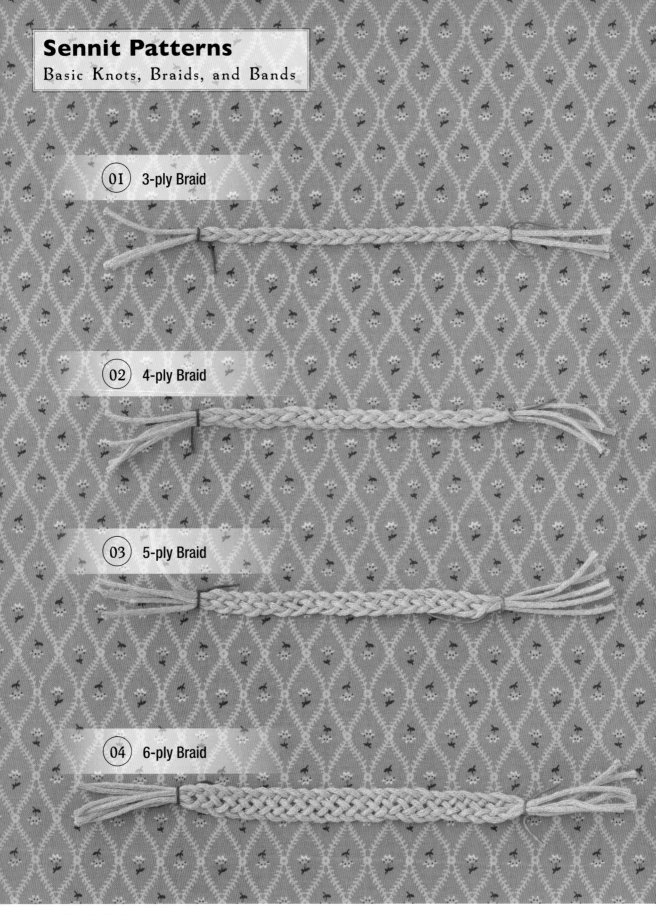

01 3-ply Braid

02 4-ply Braid

03 5-ply Braid

04 6-ply Braid

01 02 03 04 Braiding cords is just like braiding long hair. It can be done with 3 strands, or 4, 5, or more.

(05) **Square Knot**

(06) **Alternating Square Knot**

a.

b.

c.

d.

(05) **a)** The 2 working cords are the same color, the filler cords contrast. **b)** The right working cord is beige, the left working cord is white, the filler cords are brown.

(06) **c)** A total of 6 cords; the 2 filler cords contrast the 4 working cords. The offset Square Knots are alternately Left-facing and Right-facing. **d)** Same as **c)** but 2 working cords are beige, 2 are white.

29

01 3-ply Braid

This simple braiding method is familiar to almost everyone. If your cord is different on the front and back, take care that only 1 side shows.

photo page 28

I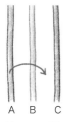
Cross cord A over cord B.

2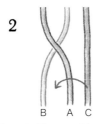
Cross cord C over cord A.

3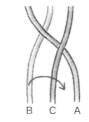
Cross cord B over cord C.

4
Continue, alternately crossing the right and left outer cords over the center cord; tighten the braid as you work.

---

02 4-ply Braid

It looks difficult at first, but once you learn how—crossing the cords in sequence "right over left" twice, and next crossing the cords then in the center "left over right"—it becomes easy.

photo page 28

I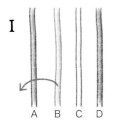
Cross cord B over cord A.

2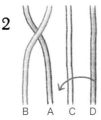
Cross cord D over cord C.

3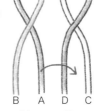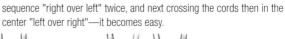
Cross cord A over cord D.

4
Continue in this manner, tightening the braid as you work.

---

03 5-ply Braid

For this braid, you first cross both outside cords toward the center, and then weave the 3 center cords as shown. Try it; practice makes it easy!

photo page 28

I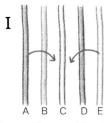
Cross cord A over cord B and cord E over cord D.

2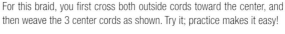
In the center, cross cord E behind cord C and then over cord A.

3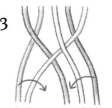
Cross cord B over cord E and cord D over cord C.

4
Continue, repeating steps 2 and 3 (don't forget, the letter IDs won't apply as the cords move); tighten the braid as you work.

---

04 6-ply Braid

Although more complex, you'll see the easy logic of this braid once you set it up. It is quite wide and is ideal for belts.

photo page 28

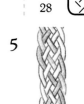

I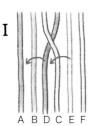
Cross cord D under cord C and then over cord B; cross cord E over cord C.

2
In the center, cross cord B over cord E.

3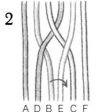
Weave both outer cords (A and F) over-and-under into the center as shown.

4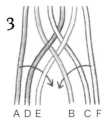
Cross the 2 cords in the center (A and F) left-over-right.

5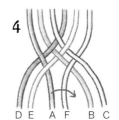
Continue, repeating steps 3 and 4 (don't forget, the letter IDs won't apply as the cords move); tighten the braid as you work.

(05) Square Knot

This is one of the most fundamental macramé knots. Tied in succession, it forms a flat chain.

photo page **29**

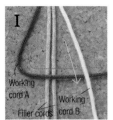

Left-facing Square Knot

Begin by pulling the left working cord (A) away from the other cords.

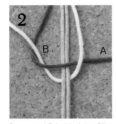

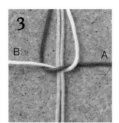

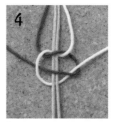

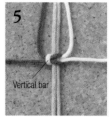

I
Bend cord A and, leaving a gap, cross it over the filler cords and then under cord B.

2
Pass cord B behind the filler cords and bring it out to the front through the left loop of cord A.

3
Gently pull cords A and B to the right and left respectively. The knot is half made.

4
Repeat steps 1–3 but reverse the way you cross the cords as shown.

5
Firmly tighten the knot. Cord B forms a vertical bar on the left edge of the sennit.

Right-facing Square Knot

Begin by pulling the right working cord (B) away from the other cords.

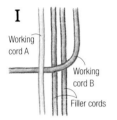

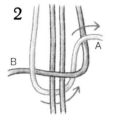

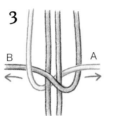

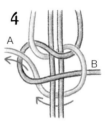

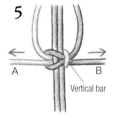

I
Bend cord B and, leaving a gap, cross it over the filler cords and then under cord A.

2
Pass cord A behind the filler cords and bring it out to the front through the right loop of cord B.

3
Gently pull cords A and B to the right and left respectively. The knot is half made.

4
Repeat steps 1–3 but reverse the way you cross the cords as shown.

5
Firmly tighten the knot. Cord A forms a vertical bar on the right edge of the sennit.

Tip-1

Which cord is next?
Whether you begin with a Left-facing or Right-facing Square Knot, when a series of Square Knots is tied, the vertical "bars" form on both edges of the sennit. It's easy to forget whether you have just tied the first or second half of your knot and thus lose track of which cord to use next. Here's a visual key: The cord coming out from under the last vertical bar is the one to bend over the filler cord next.

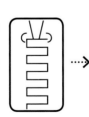 ····>

Tip-2

Make your square knotting reversible
In square knotting, the shape of the knots on the front and reverse is the same, but if the working cords are 2 different colors, one will form the vertical edge "bar" portion of the knots, the other the crossing cords, and the color placement will be reversed when you turn the work over. This photo shows the reverse of the sennit **b)** on p. 29.

(06) Alternating Square Knots

This pattern is worked with 6 cords, which are grouped differently after each knot is tied. The left 4 are knotted using Left-facing Square Knots and the right 4 knotted using Right-facing Square Knots. If cords A and B are different colors, the result will be a pattern like that **d)** on p. 29.

photo page **29**

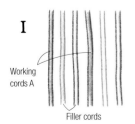

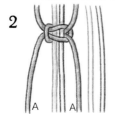

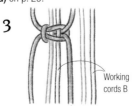

I
Begin with the left 4 cords. Of these, treat the middle 2 cords as the filler cords and the outer 2 cords as the working cords (A).

2
Tie a Left-facing Square Knot with the A cords (see above).

3
Now work with the right 4 cords, treating the middle 2 as filler cords and the outer 2 as working cords (B).

4
Tie a Right-facing Square Knot with the B cords. The sequence is complete. Repeat these 4 steps.

Chapter 02   Macramé Patterns

31

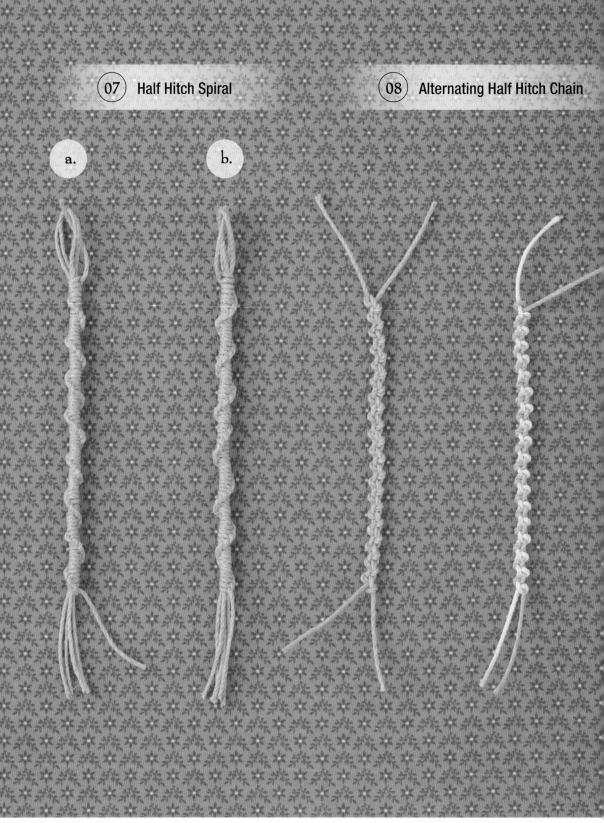

a.

b.

07 A simple knot using only 1 working cord. If you knot the working cord from the left, you get a Left-facing Half Hitch Spiral **a)**. If you knot from the right, you get a Right-facing Half Hitch Spiral **b)**.

08 A bumpy 2-cord sennit for which the left and right cords take turns being the filler cord and the working cord. Left-facing knots tied with 1 cord alternate with right-facing knots tied with the other.

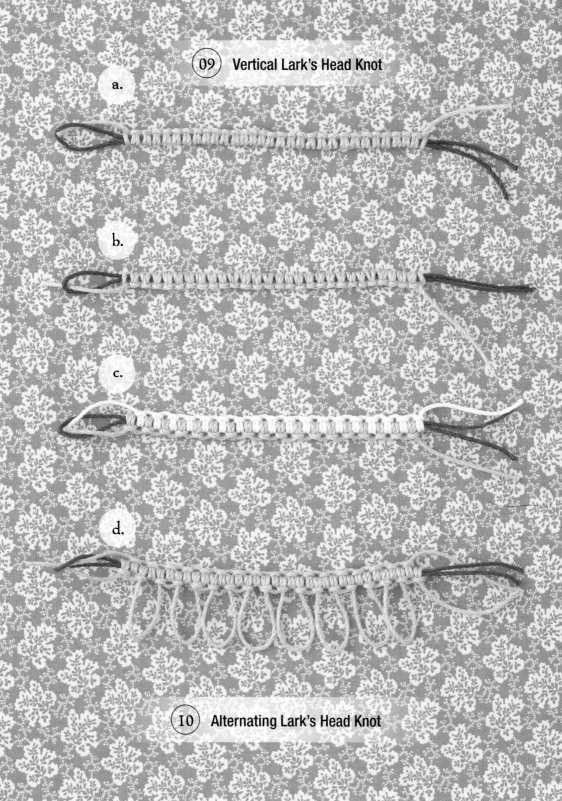

(09) Vertical Lark's Head Knot

a.

b.

c.

d.

(10) Alternating Lark's Head Knot

(09) **a)** A Right-facing Lark's Head sennit, in which a vertical "bar" forms on the right edge.
b) A Left-facing Lark's Head sennit, in which a vertical "bar" forms on the left edge.

(10) **c)** Alternating Right-facing and Left-facing Lark's Head Knots.
d) Alternating Right-facing and Left-facing Lark's Head Knots with Picots on 1 side.

07 Half Hitch Spiral

This series of simple, adjacent knots tied with a single working cord around a filler cord(s) forms a spiral because all the knots face the same way.

photo page 32

Left-facing Half Hitch

The working cord passes in front of and then ties around the filler cords from the left side, resulting in a line of bumps that spirals downward from left to right.

1

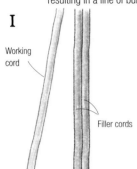

Working cord

Filler cords

Use a working cord that is 4–5 times the desired length of the finished sennit. Hold it to the left of the filler cords.

2

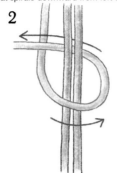

Wrap the working cord forward and then back around the filler cords; pass it through the loop on the left.

3

Pull the end of the working cord down to tighten the Left-facing Half Hitch Knot.

4

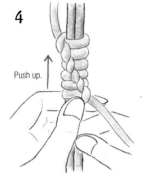

Push up.

When the knots spiral roughly halfway around the filler cord, tighten them by pushing them upward.

Right-facing Half Hitch

The working cord passes in front of and then ties around the filler cords from the right side, resulting in a line of bumps that spirals downward from right to left.

1

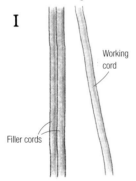

Working cord

Filler cords

Use a working cord that is 4–5 times the desired length of the finished sennit. Hold it to the right of the filler cords.

2

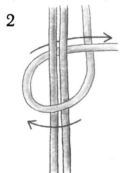

Wrap the working cord forward and then back around the filler cords; pass it through the loop on the right.

3

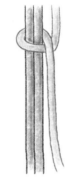

Pull the end of the working cord down to tighten the Right-facing Half Hitch Knot.

4

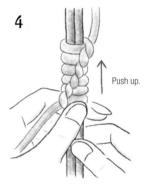

Push up.

When the knots spiral roughly halfway around the filler cord, tighten them by pushing them upward.

08 Alternating Half Hitch Chain

This is an easy textured half hitch sennit made of 2 cords; each is alternately the working cord and the filler cord.

photo page 32

1

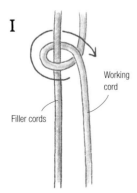

Working cord

Filler cords

To begin, use the left cord as the filler cord and tie a Right-facing Half Hitch Knot around it with the right cord.

2

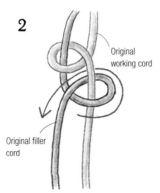

Original working cord

Original filler cord

Now switch cords and use the original filler cord to tie a Left-facing Half Hitch Knot around the original working cord.

3

The sequence is complete. Repeat steps 1 and 2 until your chain is the desired length.

Tip

The symbol tells which way the first knot faces

In the instructions on the left and the symbol above, we show the Half Hitch Chain starting from the right edge, with a Right-facing Half Hitch Knot. When you see the symbol below, you should start the sequence from the left.

Symbol for an Alternating Half Hitch chain starting from the left edge.

09   Vertical Lark's Head Knot

The Lark's Head Knot is sometimes called a Reverse Double Half Hitch. Note how the vertical bar on the edge tops both ends of the working cord.

photo page 33

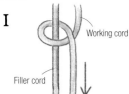

Right-facing Vertical Lark's Head Knot (a)

Use the right cord as the working cord, and work down, placing each wrap below the previous one.

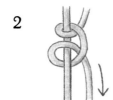

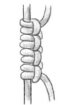

1

Wrap the working cord forward and then back around the filler cord; pass it through the loop on the right.

2

Wrap the working cord behind and then forward around the filler cord; pass it through the loop on the right.

3

Pull the working cord to tighten and complete the knot.

4

Repeat steps 1–3 until your sennit is the desired length.

Left-facing Vertical Lark's Head Knot (b)

Use the left cord as the working cord, and work down, placing each wrap below the previous one.

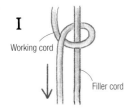

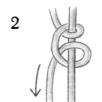

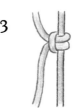

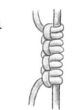

1

Wrap the working cord forward and then back around the filler cord; pass it through the loop on the left.

2

Wrap the working cord behind and then forward around the filler cord; pass it through the loop on the left.

3

Pull the working cord to tighten and complete the knot.

4

Repeat steps 1–3 until your sennit is the desired length.

10   Alternating Lark's Head Knots

When you alternate Left- and Right-facing Lark's Head Knots, small vertical bars form along both edges of the sennit.

photo page 33

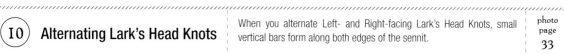

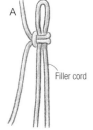

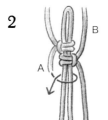

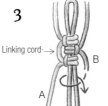

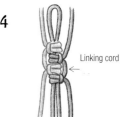

1

Tie working cord A in a Left-facing Lark's Head knot.

2

Tie working cord B in a Right-facing Lark's Head Knot. Then bring cord A below this knot and tie another Left-facing Lark's Head Knot.

3

The linking section of A should lie almost flat. Next bring working cord B below this knot and tie another Right-facing Lark's Head Knot.

4

Continue knotting in this way, making sure the linking cords lie evenly along the edges.

Tip

Make a loopy picot edge

The Alternating Lark's Head Knot sennit in **d)** on p. 33 has large loops, called picots, along 1 edge. To make a picot, all you have to do is leave extra length in the working cord between subsequent knots (noted as "linking cord" on the diagrams above), and then push the lower knot up so the link curves out.

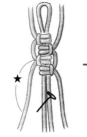

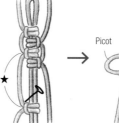

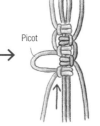

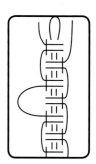

Pin down the cord at a point that is twice the length ★ of the desired picot.

Complete 1 Left-facing Lark's Head Knot.

Remove the pin, hold the filler cords, and push up the knot to create a picot.

Alternating Lark's Head with picot on left edge.

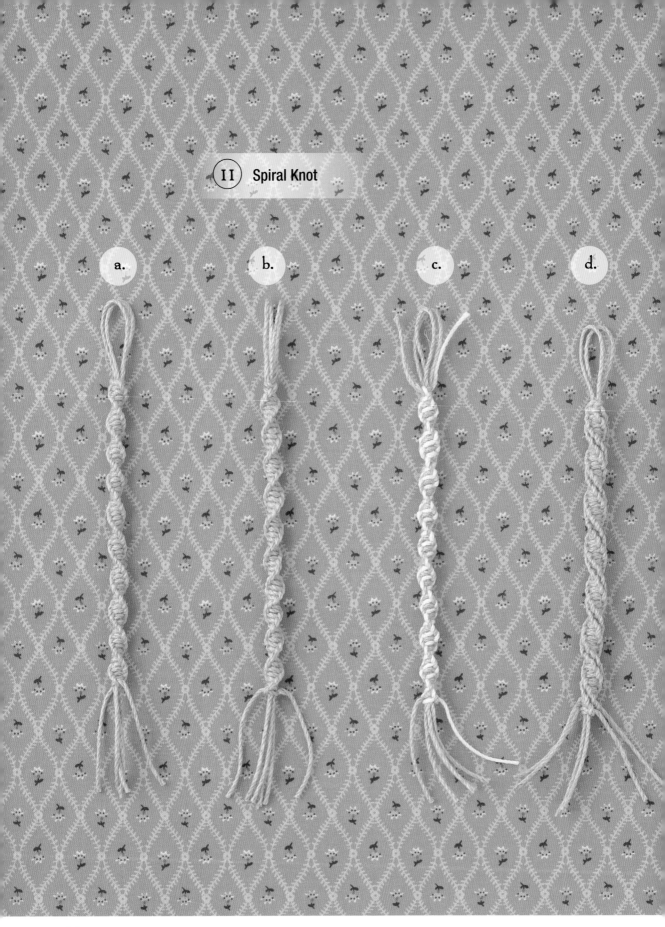

(II) Spiral Knot

a. **b.** **c.** **d.**

(II) **a)** A Left-twist Spiral is formed when the first half of a Square Knot is tied repeatedly. **b)** The Right-twist Spiral is tied from the second half of a Square Knot. **c)** Contrasting working cords create a more decorative Left-twist Spiral.

(12) **Double Spiral Knot**   (13) **Double Alternating Spiral Knot**

e.   f.   g.   h.

(12) Double Spirals are tied with 2 working cords; **d)** twists left, **e)** twists right, **f)** is made with contrasting working cords.

(13) **g)** In the Double Alternating Spiral Knot, tied with both Left-twist and Right-twist Spiral Knots, the edge bars form a diamond pattern.
h) Is made with contrasting working cords.

Also known as the Half Knot Spiral, this twisting sennit is created when just half of the Square Knot (→p. 31) is tied repeatedly.

Left-twist Spiral Knot

When the first half of the Left-Facing Square Knot is tied repeatedly, the vertical "bars" of the knot become offset, forming a spiral that twists down from left to right.

I

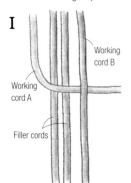

Bend cord A and, leaving a gap, cross it over the filler cords and then under cord B.

2

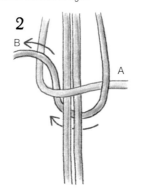

Pass cord B behind the filler cords and bring it out to the front through the left loop of cord A.

3

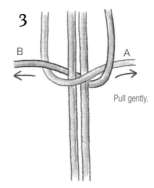

Pull cords A and B to the right and left respectively. One Spiral Knot is complete.

4

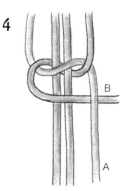

Bend cord B down and, leaving a gap, cross it over the filler cords and then under cord A.

5

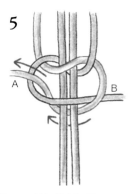

Pass cord A behind the filler cords and bring it out to the front through the left loop of cord B.

6

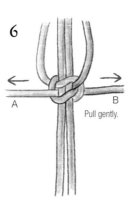

Pull cords B and A to the right and left respectively. The second Spiral Knot is complete.

7

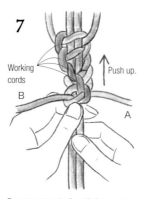

Repeat steps 1–6 until the sennit is the desired length. As the spiral forms, let the work revolve—the left and right working cords will switch positions naturally. Push the sequence of knots upward to tighten.

Tip

Turn the work, not your head

Don't worry, this knot is reversible so you can keep crossing "left over right" as the work revolves and the cords switch position—and it will be neater if you let it turn regularly.

Right-twist Spiral Knot

Similar to the Left-twist Spiral Knot, but made by repeating the first half of the Right-facing Square Knot, resulting in a spiral that twists down from right to left.

I

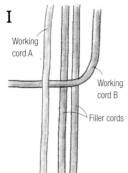

Bend cord B and, leaving a gap, cross it over the filler cords and then under cord A.

2

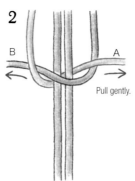

Pass cord A behind the filler cords and bright it out to the front through the right loop of cord B. Pull cords A and B evenly outwards.

3

Continue, repeating steps 1 and 2 (don't forget, the letter IDs won't apply as the cords move).

4

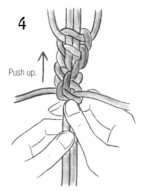

As the spiral forms, let the work revolve—the left and right working cords will switch positions naturally (see the Tip above). Push the sequence of knots upward to tighten.

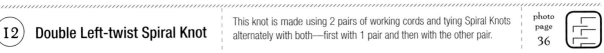

(12) Double Left-twist Spiral Knot

This knot is made using 2 pairs of working cords and tying Spiral Knots alternately with both—first with 1 pair and then with the other pair.

photo page 36

I

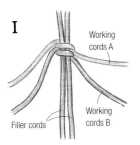

Working cords A
Filler cords
Working cords B

Tie the middle of cord A to the filler cords with an overhand knot; repeat with cord B. Make sure the knots made are behind the filler cords.

2

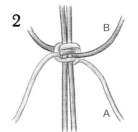

B
A

Move cord B up, out of the way, passing its right end in front of cord A and its left end behind cord A. Then with cord A, make 1 Left-twist Spiral Knot (→p. 38).

3

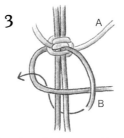

A
B

Repeat step 2 but move cord A up out of the way and tie the knot with cord B.

 Double Right-twist Spiral Knot

To make the sennet spiral from right to left, follow the steps given in this section but tie Right-twist Spiral Knots instead (→p. 38).

4

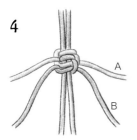

A
B

One Double Spiral Knot is complete. Repeat steps 2 and 3 until your sennit is the desired length; let the work revolve as you go.

5

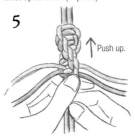

↑ Push up.

After every 4 or 5 Double Spiral Knots, hold the filler cords and push up the knots up to tighten.

Tip

2 Colors Make a Bolder Pattern

f) on p. 37 shows a Double Spiral Knot sennit in which each pair of working cords is a different color. The effect is pretty and more dramatic, with the pattern more apparent. Plus it's easier to remember which cord to use next if each is a different color.

Chapter 02 Macramé Patterns

---

(13) Double Alternating Spiral Knot

For this diamond-textured sennit, you alternately tie Right-twist and Left-twist Spiral Knots. The result is a design with 2 intersecting spirals.

photo page 37

I

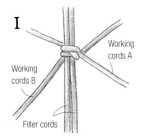

Working cords A
Working cords B
Filler cords

Attach working cords A and B to the filler cords. Adjust their position so each working cord slants diagonally as shown and their ends form an X.

2

B
A
Filler cords
Right-hand cord goes over.

Make 1 Right-twist Spiral Knot (→p. 38) with cord A.

3

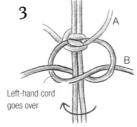

A
B
Left-hand cord goes over

Turn the whole knot slightly to the left and make 1 Left-twist Spiral Knot with cord B. One Double Alternating Spiral Knot is complete.

Tip

Count 3 Complete Double Knots

The key to making the Double Alternating Spiral Knot repeat neatly is to make sure the diamonds intersect at regular intervals. The edge bars should meet alternately at the tip or side point of the diamond every time you've completed 3 Double Alternating Spiral Knots. Practice with contrasting cords!

4

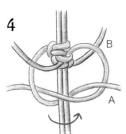

B
A

Bring the whole knot back slightly to the right, and continue, repeating steps 2 and 3 twice. Make sure the cords overlap exactly as shown as you change from A to B to A.

5

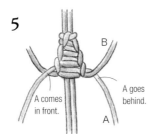

B
A comes in front.
A goes behind.
A

When the edge bars of cords A and B meet (after tying with cord B), let the work rotate until the flat space faces you and switch the orientation of the cords as shown.

6

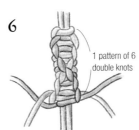

1 pattern of 6 double knots

Now tie step 3 with A and step 2 with B; repeat twice. Occasionally, hold the filler cords and push up the knots to tighten. Repeat steps 2–6.

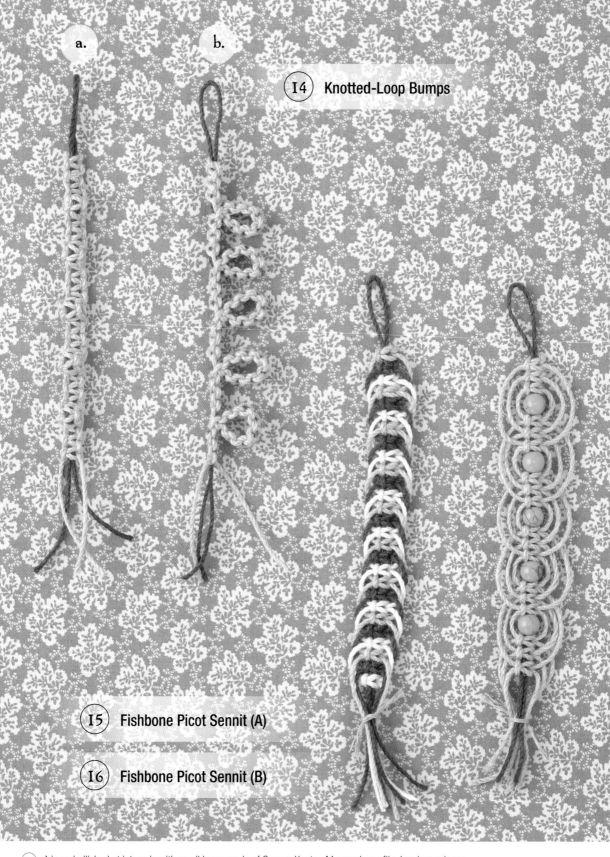

a.

b.

(14) Knotted-Loop Bumps

(15) Fishbone Picot Sennit (A)

(16) Fishbone Picot Sennit (B)

(14) **a)** is embellished at intervals with small loops made of Square Knots. **b)** seen in profile, has larger loops.

(15) and (16) feature Fishbone Picots, made when multiple working cords are tied in a repeating sequence, each carried down to enclose the next in a semicircular loop.

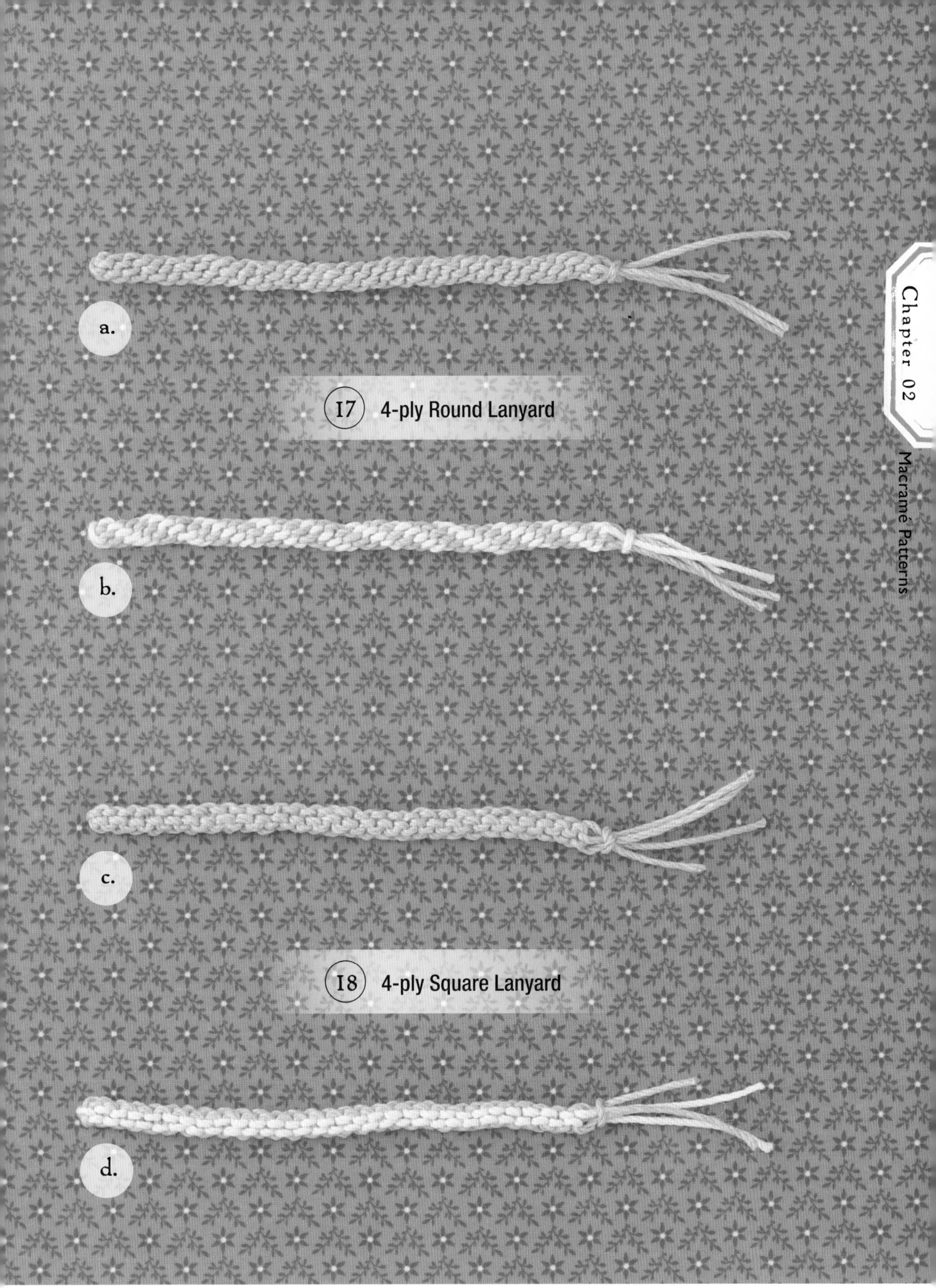

a.

17 4-ply Round Lanyard

b.

c.

18 4-ply Square Lanyard

d.

17 You can create round ropes like **a)** and **b)** with 4 cords. If you use 2 colors the surface will have a diagonal stripe.

18 A small adjustment to the braiding sequence will create a square rope: **c)** and **d)** . If you use 2 colors, the surface will have a vertical stripe.

14 Knotted-Loop Bumps

To add a button-like bump to the face of your work, simply tie several Square Knots, roll them up, and insert the cord ends back into your work.

I

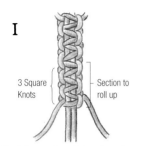

3 Square Knots · Section to roll up

Tie 3 Square Knots below the point where you want the button-like bump (→p. 31).

2

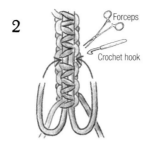

Forceps
Crochet hook

Lift the ends of the filler cords and use a forceps and crochet hook to feed them through the gaps between the filler cords and the working cords as shown.

3

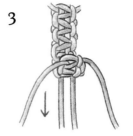

Pull down the filler cords to roll the 3-knot section into a ball.

4

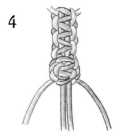

Make 1 more Square Knot below the ball to secure it.

Tip

Tie and roll more knots to make a loop

To make a knotted loop on the face of your work, simply tie and roll more Square Knots. For example, in the photo at right, the loop is made of 8 Square Knots. Experiment to find the number to tie, or use the numeral in the center of the symbol for a given project. The diagram that corresponds to the photo at right shows a sequence of 3 Left-facing Square Knots followed by a Knotted Loop of 8 Square Knots.

 Symbol for 5-Knot Loop

Symbol for 8-Knot Loop

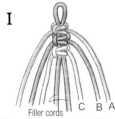 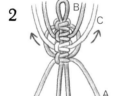 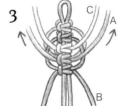   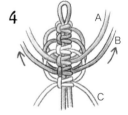

---

15 Fishbone Picot Sennit (A)

Three pairs of working cords, tied in sequence into Square Knots, leave overlapping, floating loops along the edges of your work. Flexible cords are the best choice here.

photo page 40

I

C B A
Filler cords

Make a Square Knot (→p. 31) with cords A, then cords B, then cords C.

2

Lift cords B and C up out of the way; bring cords A down behind them, creating a semicircular loop on each edge of the work, and tie in a Square Knot.

3

 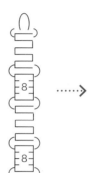

Lift cords C and A up out of the way; bring cords B down behind and tie in a Square Knot, leaving loops as in step 2.

4

Lift cords A and B up out of the way; bring cords C down behind and tie in a Square Knot, leaving loops as in step 2. Repeat steps 2–4 until the sennit is the desired length.

---

16 Fishbone Picot Sennit (B)

This variation changes the Fishbone knotting sequence so the Picots create concentric circles. You can string a bead in the center of the pattern if you like.

photo page 40

I

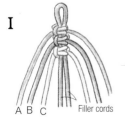

A B C
Filler cords

Make a Square Knot (→p. 31) with cords A, then cords B, then cords C.

2

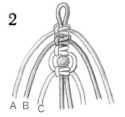

A B C

String a bead onto the filler cords. Bring cords C down, creating a small semicircular loop on each edge of the work, and tie in a Square Knot.

3

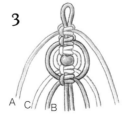

A C B

Brings cords B down in front, creating a medium semicircular loop on each edge of the work, and tie in a Square Knot.

4

C B A

Brings cords A down in front, creating a large semicircular loop on each edge of the work, and tie in a Square Knot. Continue in this manner, always using the inner cords to make the first knot after adding another bead.

17 4-ply Round Lanyard

In this technique, 4 cords are overlapped in sequence to create a parallel cross pattern. The direction of the overlap is consistent and forms a diagonal pattern on the rope surface.

photo page 41

1

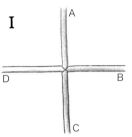

Begin with 4 cords, each 4–5 times the desired length of the finished piece; arrange them end-to-end to form a cross as shown. (Or overlap 2 cords, each 10 times the finished length.)

2

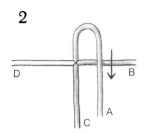

Fold cord A over cord B.

3

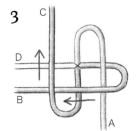

Fold cord B over cord C, and cord C over cords B and D.

4

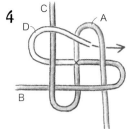

Fold cord D over cord C and then through the loop created by cord A.

5

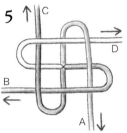

One at a time, gently pull the end of each cord to tighten the knot.

6

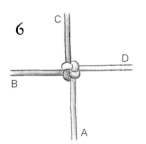

One knot of the 4-ply Round Lanyard is complete.

7

Repeat steps 2–5 until the lanyard is the desired length (always begin with the cord that points north; the letter IDs won't apply as the cords move).

Tip

Create diagonal stripes

In **b)** on p. 41, cords A and C are beige and cords B and D are white. When you use 2 colors like this, you create a diagonally striped lanyard that looks a bit like a barbershop pole.

---

18 4-ply Square Lanyard

Similar to the Four-ply Round Lanyard, but after each knot, you reverse the direction in which you overlap the cords, creating a square rope with a vertical texture.

photo page 41

1

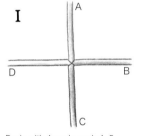

Begin with 4 cords, each 4–5 times the desired length of the finished piece; arrange them end-to-end to form a cross as shown. (Or overlap 2 cords, each 10 times the finished length.)

2

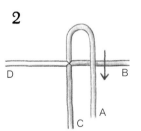

Follow steps 2–5 of Four-ply Round Lanyard (above) to make the first knot.

3

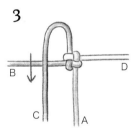

To begin the second knot, reverse the direction and fold cord C over cord B.

4

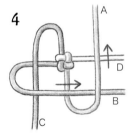

Fold cord B over cord C and cord A over cords B and D.

5

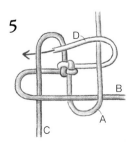

Fold cord D over cord C and through the loop created by cord C.

6

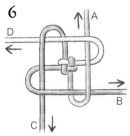

One at a time, gently pull the end of each cord to tighten the knot.

7

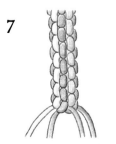

Repeat steps 2–6 until the lanyard is the desired length.

Tip

Create Vertical Stripes

For **d)** on p. 41, cords A and C are beige and cords B and D are white. These are the same colors as in **b)**, but with the 4-ply Square Lanyard the folded cords align in vertical stripes.

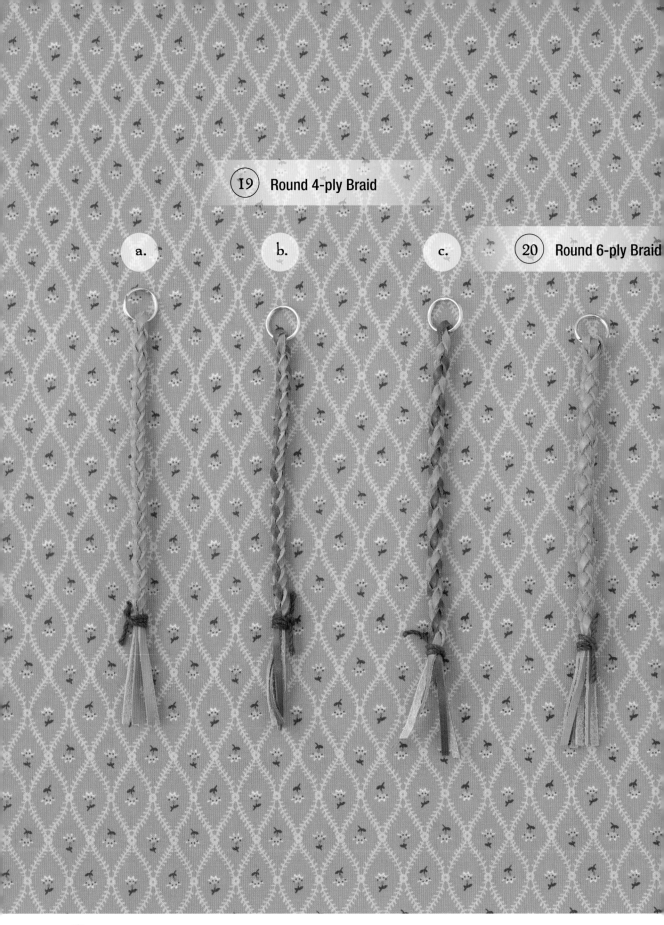

19 Round 4-ply Braid

a. **b.** **c.** 20 Round 6-ply Braid

19 These multi-cord braids are great for small leather items. Use 2 colors to create a vertical stripe, as in **b)**, or a diagonal stripe, as in **c)**.

20 Six cords create a thicker braid. If you use a round cord instead of a flat one, the effect will be slightly different.

21 Square Herringbone Braid

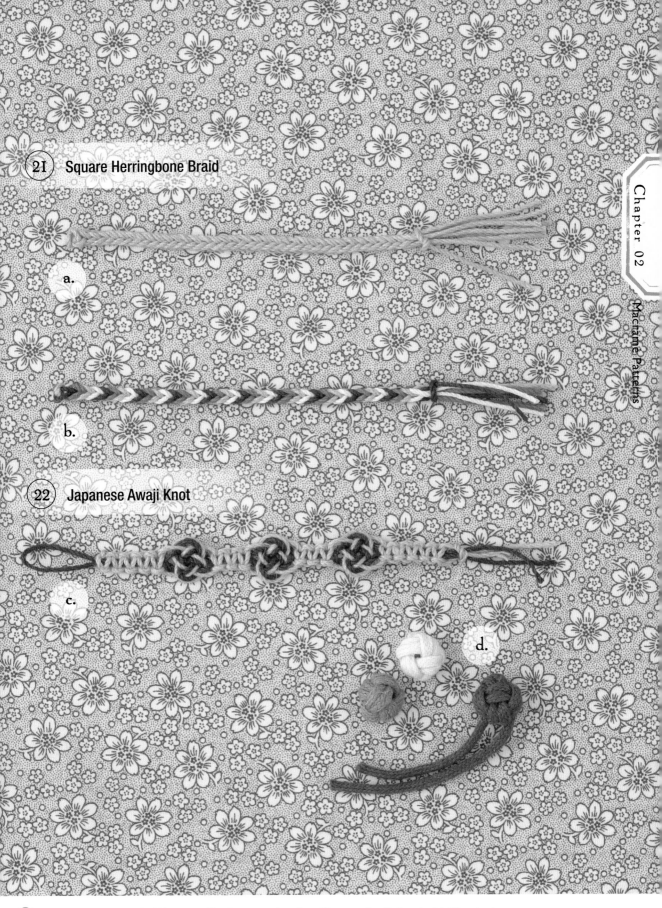

a.

b.

22 Japanese Awaji Knot

c.

d.

21 This tight, 8-cord square braid has a neat V pattern on each surface. **b)** was made with 2 each of 4 different colors.

22 A decorative Awaji Knot made with 2 cords has been added at intervals to a Square Knot sinnet. The same knot, made from 1 cord, has been tightened into a ball **d)**.

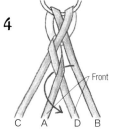
(19) Round 4-ply Braid

For this 4-ply braiding technique you wrap the outside cords in alternating sequence around the 2 inside cords. The trick: the cord currently not in use is the one to use next.

I

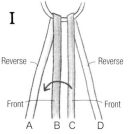

Begin with 2 cords, each about 2½ times the desired length of the finished piece; fold each in half over a ring. (Or use 4 cords, each about 1¼ times the desired finished length.) Cross cord C over cord B.

2

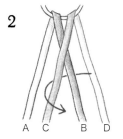

Follow the arrow to wrap cord D behind cords B and C; then wrap forward and place between them.

3

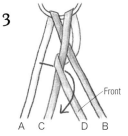

Follow the arrow to wrap cord A behind cords C and D; then wrap forward and place between them.

4

Follow the arrow to wrap cord B behind cords D and A; then wrap forward and place between them.

5

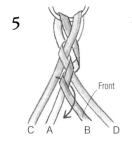

Follow the arrow to wrap cord C behind cords A and B; then wrap forward and place between them.

6

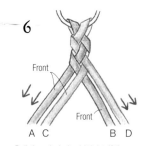

Pull the whole braid tight. If the cords have a front and reverse, adjust them so the fronts face out.

7

Continue braiding, repeating steps 2–6 (don't forget, the letter IDs won't apply as the cords move).

Tip

Use 2 colors for effect

For this 4-ply Braid you can create a diagonal stripe pattern by using 1 color for cords A and B, and a different color for cords C and D, as in **c)** on p. 44. If you make A and C a single color, and cords B and D a different color, your braid will have straight, vertical stripe as in **b)** on p. 44.

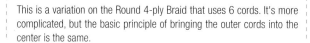

(20) Round 6-ply Braid

This is a variation on the Round 4-ply Braid that uses 6 cords. It's more complicated, but the basic principle of bringing the outer cords into the center is the same.

photo page 44

I

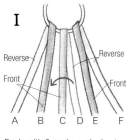

Begin with 3 cords, each about 2½ times the desired length of the finished piece; fold each in half over a ring. (Or use 6 cords, each about 1¼ times the desired finished length.) Cross cord C over cord D.

2

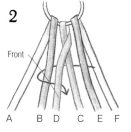

Follow the arrow to wrap cord F behind cords E, C, D, and B; then wrap forward around B, under D, and out between D and C.

3

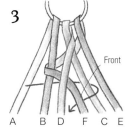

Follow the arrow to wrap A behind B, D, F, and C; then wrap forward around C, under F, and out between D and F.

4

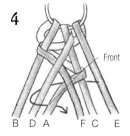

Follow the arrow to wrap cord E as shown.

5

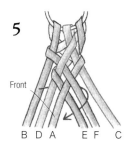

Follow the arrow to wrap cord B as shown.

6

Follow the arrow to wrap cord C as shown.

7

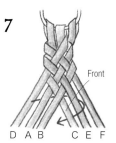

Follow the arrow to wrap cord D as shown.

8

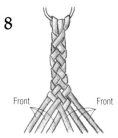

Pull the whole braid tight. If the cords have a front and reverse, adjust them so the fronts face out. Repeat steps 2–7 until the braid is the desired length.

21 Square Herringbone Braid

Here 8 cords braided together make a square rope patterned with nested Vs on the front and back, inverted Vs on the sides. Label the cord ends to keep them straight.

photo page **45**

I

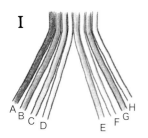

Align 8 cords side-by-side, grouping 4 on the left and 4 on the right.

2

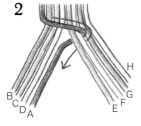

Follow the arrow to wrap cord A over and then behind cords F and E, bringing it to rest to the right of cord D. Pull to tighten.

3

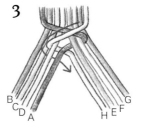

Follow the arrow to wrap cord H over and then behind cords D and A, bring it to rest to the left of cord E. Pull to tighten.

4

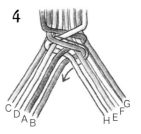

Wrap cord B over and then behind cords H and E, bringing it to rest to the right of cord A. Pull to tighten.

5

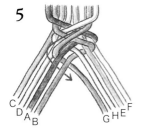

Wrap cord G over then behind cords A and B, bringing it to rest to the left of cord H. Pull to tighten.

6

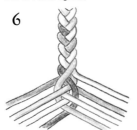

Keep braiding like this from alternate edges, lifting the outermost cord on 1 edge and wrapping it down between the second and third cords of the opposite group.

7

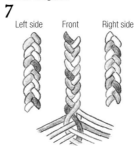

Left side · Front · Right side

Eventually, the whole braid will become square, with the nested Vs pointing up or down on alternate sides.

Tip

4 colors make a striking pattern

In **b)** on p. 45, 4 colors were used for the Square Herringbone Braid, paired as follows: A and H, B and G, C and F, and D and E. By making it this way, we created a dramatic featherlike pattern. Try it, using colors that you like.

22 Japanese Awaji Knot

This decorative knot is also known as a Double Coin Knot and Josephine Knot. It can be made with a single cord, but 2 parallel cords make it more impressive.

photo page **45**

I

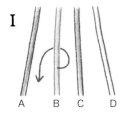

Follow the path of the arrow to form a loose loop with cord B.

2

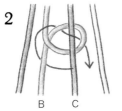

Follow the path of the arrow to form another loop with cord C, weaving it under and over and through as shown.

3

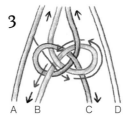

Adjust the loops to have a nice form but don't tighten them. Now weave cord A through the knot alongside cord B.

4

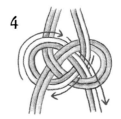

Weave cord D alongside cord C. Adjust the final shape so the cords lie smoothly together.

Tip

Make an Awaji Knot Ball

If you use a single cord to trace the path of the Awaji knot twice and then tighten it, you can make a cute knotted ball, like the one in **d)** on p. 45. Use it as button or a bead.

①

②

③ 4th loop

④

⑤

⑥ Push up.

⑦

⑧ Cut.

① Fold a single cord loosely in half and use the ends to follow steps 1–3 of Awaji Knot (above).

②③ Now weave the B end of the cord through the knot again, creating a 4th loop at the bottom and then placing the B cord alongside the previous cord.

④ Finally, follow the path of the arrow to insert the B end of the cord from the front to the back of the knot.

⑤ Pull both the ends of the cord to tighten the knot from the starting point to the finishing point, adjusting so that there are no gaps.

⑥ Push the center of the knot up with your fingers to start forming a ball.

⑦ Gradually pull the ends to tighten any loose areas on the inside and keep forming a ball.

⑧ Once the ball is tight and round, cut off the ends of the cords flush with the surface; seal the cord ends with glue.

1-Knot Buttons and Balls

Fun Embellishments to Make with a Single Knot

There are many other decorative knots similar to the Awaji Knot (introduced on p. 45) that can be made into balls or flower-like motifs. They can be used on their own to decorate straps or key chains, or the ends can be finished neatly to create buttons and brooches, or they can be attached to clothing and bags as a decorative accent—whatever you fancy. You can even make lots of colorful balls and string them together to make a necklace or bracelet.

So choose your favorite type of cord and color and have some fun!

A French Knot Button

B Lucky Knot Button

C Monkey First Knot Button

A tassel charm made with a French Knot over filler cords.

A clip-on charm made with Monkey First Knots.

How to Knot Buttons and Balls

Basic 4-cord French Knot

The French Knot creates a decorative finish at the end of a braid and is often used as a design accent.

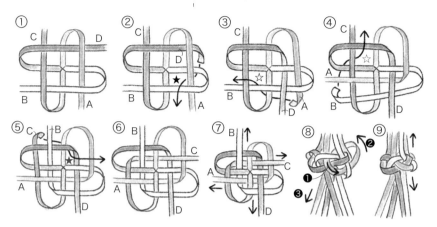

① Complete the first 4 steps of the Round 4-ply Rope (→p. 43).

② Pass cord D from behind to the front through the loop marked ★.

③ Pass cord A from behind to the front through the loop marked ☆.

④ Pass cord B from behind to the front through the loop marked ☆ (red).

⑤ Pass cord C from behind to the front through the loop marked ★ (red).

⑥ Make sure all the cords are coming out from the central point facing upwards.

⑦ One at a time, gently pull the end of each cord to tighten the knot.

⑧ Use an awl to gently tease the looseness from the center to the ends of the cords, and pull the knot once again to tighten.

⑨ Pull upward and downward to adjust the shape of the knot.

Basic Monkey Fist Knot

This popular knot resembles the fist of a monkey—hence its name. A small ball or a bead placed in the center helps to build its shape.

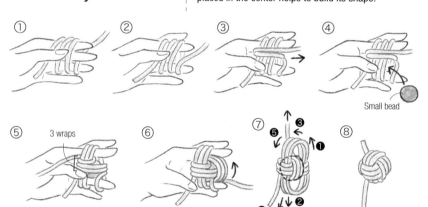

Small bead

3 wraps

① Wrap a cord 3 times around your first 3 fingers.

② Pull out your middle finger.

③ Through the space between the remaining 2 fingers, wrap the end of the cord twice around the 3 vertical wraps, as shown. (You may find this easier using a yarn needle.)

④ Insert a small ball, bead, or rolled up piece of foil into the center.

⑤ Wrap the end of the cord once more around the 3 vertical wraps.

⑥ Now wrap the end of the cord 3 times vertically around the 3 horizontal wraps as shown.

⑦ Remove the wraps from your fingers. Pull tight in sequence as shown.

⑧ The Monkey Knot is complete.

Lucky Knot

As its name suggests, this decorative knot is used in Asia as a token that brings good fortune. Its shape is made by stretching out the loops at the top and bottom, left and right.

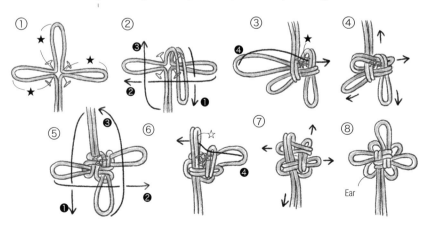

Ear

① Fold a single cord in half and then fold each end again, forming 3 equal loops as shown; pin down at the center. The ★ indicates your chosen measurement.

② Follow the numbered arrows in sequence to fold the loops and bottom cords.

③ Fold over loop 4 and pull it through the loop indicated by the ★.

④ To tighten the center, gently pull the loops as shown by the arrows.

⑤ Follow the numbered arrows in sequence to fold the loops and top cords (in reverse of step 2).

⑥ Fold over loop 4 and pull it through the loop indicated by the ☆.

⑦ Remove pins and gently pull the loops as shown by the arrows.

⑧ Now pull out the little "ears" and adjust the shape to complete the knot.

1-knot Buttons (photos page 48)

materials

A French Knot Button

For each button: 2 flat leather cords (5mm diameter), each 12"/30cm long

    (top) 1 cord each Red and White
    (left) 1 cord each Natural and Brown
    (right) 1 cord each Natural and Green

B Lucky Knot Button

For each button, 1 piece round leather cord (2mm diameter), 30"/75cm long

    (top) Sand
    (right) Dark Red
    (bottom) Dark Green

1 small metal ring to be the shank for each button

C Monkey Fist Button

For each button, 1 piece round leather cord (2mm diameter), 28"/70cm long

    (top) Aged Natural
    (left) Dark Red
    (right) Caramel

1 round wood bead (8mm diameter) for inserting into the knot

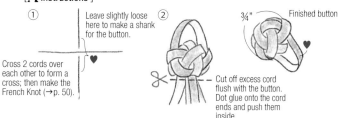

[A Instructions]

① Leave slightly loose here to make a shank for the button.

Cross 2 cords over each other to form a cross; then make the French Knot (→p. 50).

②

¾" Finished button

Cut off excess cord flush with the button. Dot glue onto the cord ends and push them inside.

[B Instructions]

① ⅜" ⅜" ⅜"

Set up your cord as shown; then make the Lucky Knot (→p. 50).

② Wrong side

A B

Make a loop.

Turn the knot wrong side up; cut excess cord B flush with the edge of the knot. Thread cord A through the knot, making a loop below; then cut off the excess.

③ Wrong side

1⅜"

Glue or sew a small metal ring to the center for a button shank.

[C Instructions]

① Make a Monkey Fist Knot (→p. 50).

② ¾"

To make a button shank, cut off 1 cord above the knot as shown and fold the extension into a loop; glue the end to the knot.

③ ⅝"

Cut the other extending cord flush with the surface of the knot.

French Knot Tassel Charm (photo page 49)

materials

(for each tassel)

2 flat leather cords (5mm diameter), each 12"/30cm long

    (left) 1 cord each Natural and Red
    (right) 1 cord each Red and White

5 pieces Jute Ramie cord, each 10"/25cm long

    (left) Natural
    (right) White

One metal split ring

[Instructions]

Split ring

① Insert the 5 jute ramie cords through the split ring, folding in half to make 10 strands.

Measure from here

⅝"

② With 2 leather cords, tie a French Knot (→p. 50) around the jute cords. Trim the leather cord ends and secure them with glue.

Knot around the filler cords.

2¾"

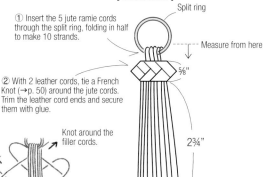

③ Trim the ends of the jute tassel cords to be even.

Monkey Fist Knot Clip-on Charm (photo page 49)

materials

Round leather cord (2mm diameter)

    2 pieces Sand, each 28"/70cm long
    1 piece Dark Red, 31½"/80cm long

1 trigger hook key chain fitting

3 round wood beads (8 mm diameter) for inserting into the knots

[Instructions]

Key chain fitting

④ Insert the ends of the cords through the ring section of the clasp; fold them over so they overlap the braid.

⑤ Use the red cord to secure the cords with a Wrapping Knot (→p. 22). Trim the ends of the cords next to the wrap.

⅜"

③ Make a 3-ply Braid, about 2¾"/7cm long, above the tying knot (→p. 30).

2"

② Lay the 3 cords side-by-side; then tie them together with the red cord.

① Make a Monkey Fist Knot from each cord (→p. 50); trim off the excess of the shorter end close to the knot.

1½"

Measure from here

Panel Patterns
Buddhist Treasure Mesh Patterns

23 Buddhist Treasure Mesh A (1 knot)

24 Buddhist Treasure Mesh B (1½ knots)

23 A tight mesh made with single Square Knots, offset on alternating rows.

24 An open mesh similar to the first, but made with 1½ Square Knots at each interval. Derived from a traditional Asian pattern of overlapping coin motifs, it is considered auspicious.

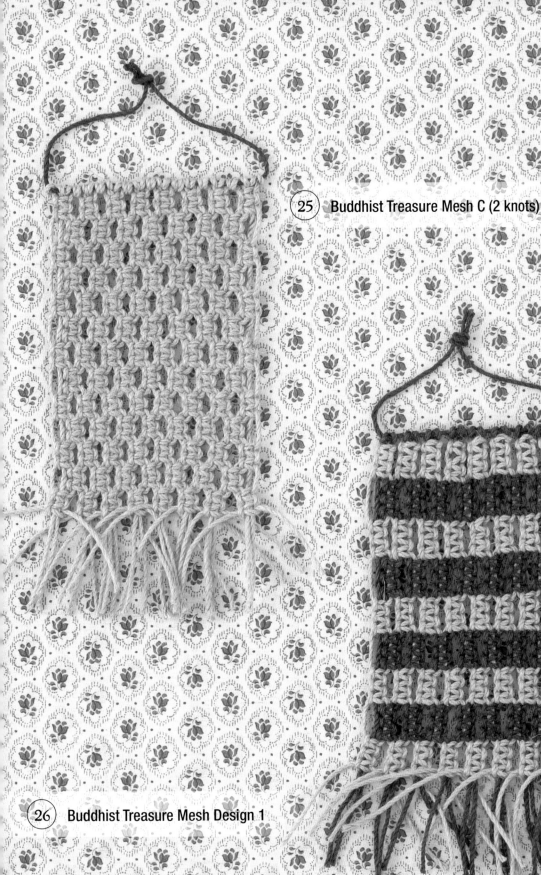

(25) **Buddhist Treasure Mesh C (2 knots)**

(26) **Buddhist Treasure Mesh Design 1**

(25) When you increase the number of Square Knots tied at each interval, the holes of the mesh take on an elongated hexagon shape.

(26) When the working cords are 2 different colors, with each used alternately to tie a row of knots, horizontal stripes grace the mesh.

(23) Buddhist Treasure Mesh A (1 knot)

This very basic mesh pattern is a simple repeat of Square Knots, spaced quite tightly and with alternate rows offset by 2 cords.

photo page 52

🌸 Knotting Diagram

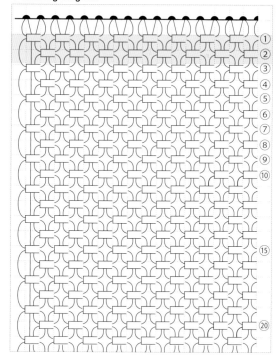

Knotting Technique

 Left-facing Square Knot → page 31

Diagram

1

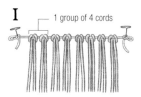

1 group of 4 cords

Tie working cords to the anchor cord in groups of 4 (4 single cords or 2 doubled cords).

2

For the first row, tie a Square Knot on each group of 4 cords.

3

For the second row, skip the first 2 cords; then tie a Square Knot on each subsequent group of 4 cords.

4

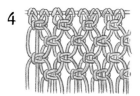

Repeat steps 1–2 until the panel is the desired length. End by repeating row 1 (so the cords at the edges are knotted).

---

(24) Buddhist Treasure Mesh B (1½ knots)

Similar to (23) above. Leave a little space between each group of 4 cords. Tie 1½ Square Knots at each position. Space the rows at larger intervals.

photo page 52

🌸 Knotting Diagram

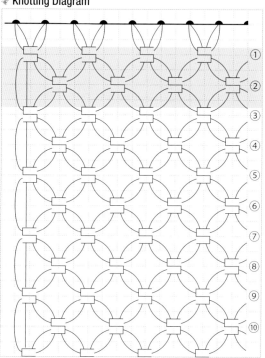

Knotting Technique

 Left-facing Square Knot → page 31

Tip

Keep the mesh uniform

Buddhist Treasure Mesh patterns get their name from the Shippo pattern of interlocking circles found in Sashiko embroidery. The key to knotting them is to achieve balance and evenness in the spacing. To regulate the space between rows, pin the piece to a knotting board, as shown at right. When you create an open mesh like this one, the Square Knots can become slack, so keep an eye on your tension to make them consistent.

(25) Buddhist Treasure Mesh C (2 knots)

Also similar to ㉓ at left, but 2 Square Knots are tied at every interval. Keep the tension very firm.

photo page 53

❧ Knotting Diagram

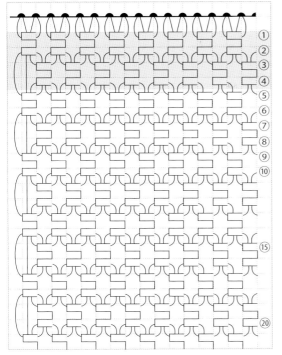

Knotting Technique

 Left-facing Square Knot → page 31

 Tip

Use Left- or Right-facing Knots consistently

For the Buddhist Treasure Mesh Patterns introduced in this book, we call for the Left-Facing Square Knot. If you use the Right-Facing Square Knot instead, the mesh will be almost identical, as shown at right. As long as the direction of the knots is the same throughout the piece, the pattern will be fine. So use the knot direction that works best for you.

---

(26) Buddhist Treasure Mesh Design 1

Here each group of 4 cords consists of 2 each of 2 contrast colors (see the Tip below to begin). Three Square Knots are tied at every interval. Switch the knot colors every 3 rows.

photo page 53

❧ Knotting Diagram

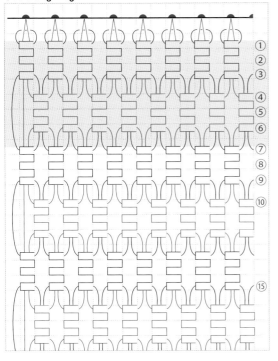

Knotting Technique

 Left-facing Square Knot → page 31

 Tip

How to attach the cords when you use 2 colors

To set up a 2-color group of 4 cords, first attach 2 cords of 1 color to the anchor cord, these form the 2 inner cords of the group in the first row of knots. Repeat across the anchor cord. Then tie 2 cords of the second color to each group, right below the anchor cord as shown (this is neatest if you use 1 long cord and tie it on at its midpoint).

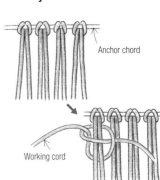

Anchor chord

Working cord

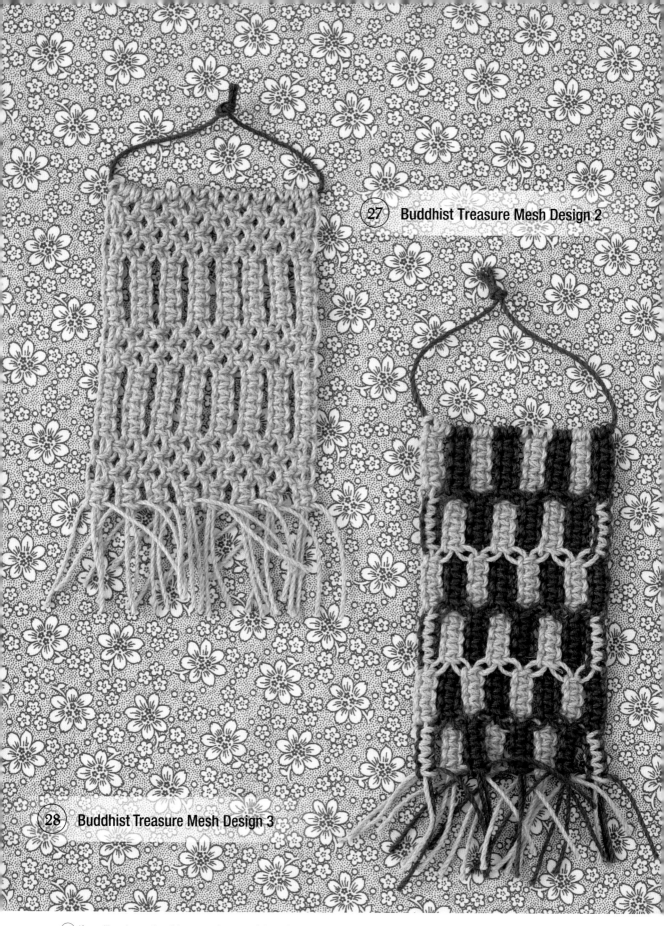

27 **Buddhist Treasure Mesh Design 2**

28 **Buddhist Treasure Mesh Design 3**

27 If you like, decorative ribbons can be passed through the long vertical gaps between the Square Knot sennits in this design.

28 This pattern looks complex, but it's made entirely of Square Knot sennits. It's because patterns like this are so easy that macramé is so wonderful!

(29) Treasure Mesh Design 4

(30) Treasure Mesh Design 5

(29) A variation on (23) Buddhist Treasure Mesh A, this pattern is more open because half the knots are skipped on every second row.

(30) In this design, 1 color is knotted in an open Buddhist Treasure Mesh A, and then the second color is woven diagonally through the mesh.

(27) Buddhist Treasure Mesh Design 2

For this pattern, we alternate several rows of Buddhist Treasure Mesh with several rows of Square Knot sennits to create a new design.

photo page 56

🪡 Knotting Diagram

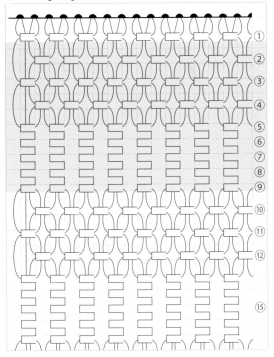

Knotting Technique

 Left-facing Square Knot → page 31

Tip

Use the space between sennits as eyelets

The use of Square Knot sennits in this design is attractive and also practical. For example, you can weave cord or tape through the gaps—as decoration or even to make a drawstring. You can adjust the number of rows of Square Knots in the sennits to accommodate your chosen cord, tape or decorative ribbon.

---

(28) Buddhist Treasure Mesh Design 3

This is a mesh of 4-row Square Knot sennits followed by crisscrossed working cords. We alternated 2 colors for the sennits.

photo page 56

🪡 Knotting Diagram

Knotting Technique

Left-facing Square Knot → page 31

Instructions

1

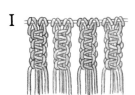

Set up the working cords in groups of 4, alternating the color from group to group. Make a sennit of 4 Left-facing Square Knots with each group.

2

Lift out of the way.

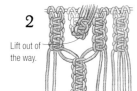

Lift the second sennit out of the way. Use the right 2 cords of the first sennit and the left 2 cords of the third sennit to make a new Square Knot sennit.

3

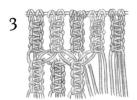

Lay the lifted sennit back down. Divide its cords; also divide the cords of the fourth sennit in the first row. Make 2 new Square Knot sennits as shown.

4

Continue in this way across the panel. Then repeat steps 2–4 until the panel is the desired length.

29 Buddhist Treasure Mesh Design 4

Each row of this pattern is tied with Square Knots, but on alternate rows, the knots are offset and every other group of 4 cords is left untied, creating a diagonal lattice. The pattern repeats every 4 rows.

photo page 57

🌸 Knotting Diagram

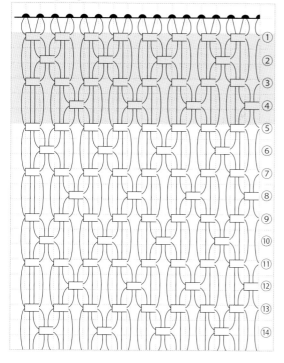

Knotting Technique

Left-facing Square Knot → page 31

Instructions

1 Set up the working cords in groups of 4. For the first row, tie a Square Knot on each group of 4 cords.

2 For the second row, leave the 2 cords at the left edge unknotted. Tie a Square Knot on the next 4 cords and then on every second group of 4 cords.

Leave. Square Knot Leave.

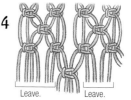

3 For the third row, begin at the edge and tie a Square Knot on every group of 4 cords (as in row 1).

4 For the fourth row, leave the first 6 cords unknotted. Tie a Square Knot on the next 4 cords and then on every second group of 4 cords. Then repeat the knotting in steps 1–4 until your panel is the desired length.

Leave. Leave.

---

30 Buddhist Treasure Mesh Design 5

The open mesh that is the base of this design is the same as ㉓ but worked on alternate groups of 4 cords. Then the unknotted cords are woven diagonally through the mesh, creating a pattern of birds in flight. Choosing a boldly contrasting color scheme is key.

photo page 57

🌸 Knotting Diagram

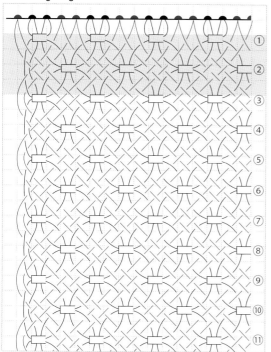

Knotting Technique

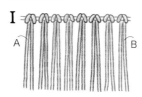

Left-facing Square Knot → page 31

Instructions

1 Set up the working cords in groups of 4, alternating the colors (A and B) from group to group (but begin and end with a group of 2 cords in B).

A   B

2 Lift all color B cords out of the way. Work 1 row of Square Knots across the panel on the color A cords as shown. Now re-divide the cords and work a row of knots offset from the first, as shown. Repeat until the panel is the desired length.

Lift out of the way.

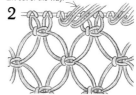

3 Follow the diagram to weave the B cords through the mesh, threading each in a yarn needle.

4 Depending on the size of your panel, you may prefer to do all the knotting at once or in stages alternating with the weaving.

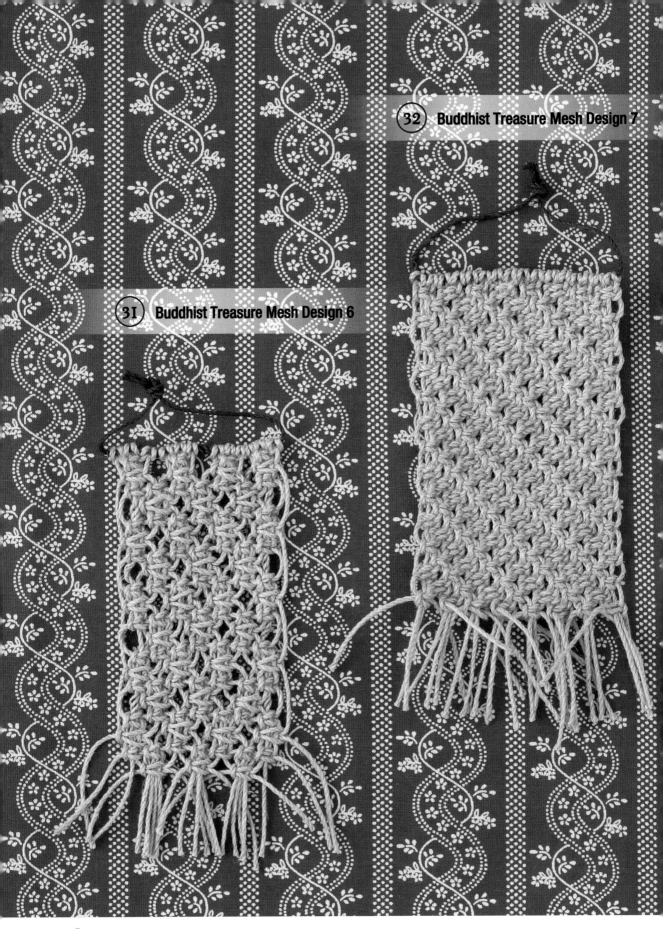

31 Buddhist Treasure Mesh Design 6

32 Buddhist Treasure Mesh Design 7

㉛ This rustic mesh is worked with groups of 6 cords, with Square Knots tied over 2, then 4, then 2 filler cords at each interval.

㉜ In this mesh Spiral Knots alternate with Square Knots in every row.

34 Buddhist Treasure Mesh with Spiral Sennits

33 Twisted Buddhist Treasure Mesh

33 Use Spiral Knots instead of Square Knots for this version of Buddhist Treasure Mesh.

34 Similar to 27 Buddhist Treasure Mesh Design 2, but the sennit bands are tied in Spiral Knots to give them a wave-like form.

31 Buddhist Treasure Mesh Design 6

By regularly changing the number of filler cords over which you tie the knots, you can create an unusual textured mesh. Set up your work with groups of 6 cords.

photo page 60

❋ Knotting Diagram

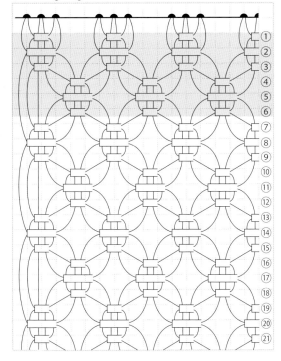

①
②
③
④
⑤
⑥
⑦
⑧
⑨
⑩
⑪
⑫
⑬
⑭
⑮
⑯
⑰
⑱
⑲
⑳
㉑

Knotting Technique

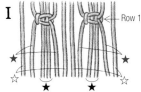 Left-facing Square Knot → page 31

Instructions

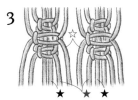

I ← Row 1

For rows 1 and 3, in each group of 6 cords, use the cords marked ★(red) to tie over the cords marked ★. For row 2, tie with the cords marked ☆ over all 4 center cords.

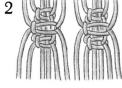

2

The finished knot sequence looks like this.

3

Repeat this sequence but offset the knots: For rows 4 and 6, first tie over adjacent ☆ cords with ★(red) cords as shown; for row 5 tie with ★ cords.

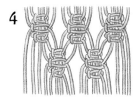

4

Repeat steps 1–3 until your panel is the desired length.

---

32 Buddhist Treasure Mesh Design 7

Set up the working cords in groups of 4. Make a Square Knot on the first group, then 2 Spiral Knots on the second group. Repeat across each row, offsetting every second row as shown.

photo page 60

❋ Knotting Diagram

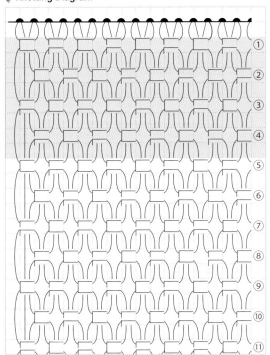

①
②
③
④
⑤
⑥
⑦
⑧
⑨
⑩
⑪

Knotting Technique

 Left-facing Square Knot → page 31

 Left-facing Spiral Knot → page 38

Tip

Try this mesh using 2 colors

If you set up your work by alternating a pair of cords of 1 color with a pair of a different color, you will create a slightly mysterious pattern like this, because the cords rotate as the Spiral Knots are tied, with unexpected results. This is one of the things that makes macramé so interesting.

(33) Twisted Buddhist Treasure Mesh

If you replace all the Square Knots in the basic Buddhist Treasure Mesh ㉓ with Spiral Knots, you create a thick fabric, perfect for making into mats.

photo page 61

❀ Knotting Diagram

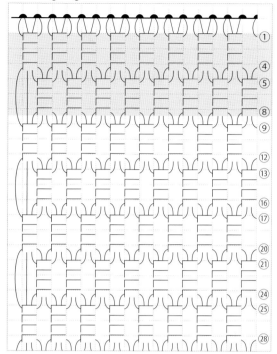

Knotting Technique

 Left-facing Spiral Knot → page 38

Tip

Make the mesh open or tight

The size of the open spaces in this mesh is controlled by the number of Spiral Knots tied on each set of cords in each row. The diagram at left shows sennits of 4 spiral knots tied on each set of cords in each row. You could tie more or fewer; however, if you use too few, a proper spiral will not form and you will end up with a weirdly twisted and unstable surface. The trick is to tie enough Spiral Knots to form a half or full spiral.

(34) Buddhist Treasure Mesh with Spiral Sennits

This panel features bands of Buddhist Treasure Mesh A ㉓ alternating with bands of Spiral Knot sennits. You may vary the length of the Spiral Knot sennit bands as you wish.

photo page 61

❀ Knotting Diagram

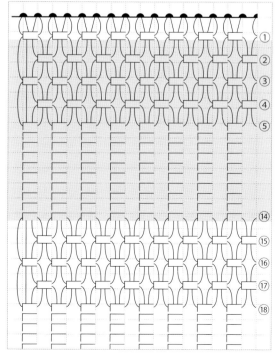

Knotting Technique

 Left-facing Square Knot → page 31

Left-facing Spiral Knot → page 38

Tip

Spiral Knots require longer working cords

When you set up your cords, make sure the cords that will be used to tie the Spiral Knot Sennits are half again as long as their filler cords — you can trace the path in the diagram at left. Refer to the drawing at right to see how the first and fourth cords (B) in every group of 4 are 1½ times the length of the second and third cords (A) in the group.

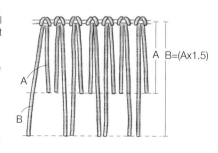

A   B=(Ax1.5)

Versatile Clove Hitch Patterns

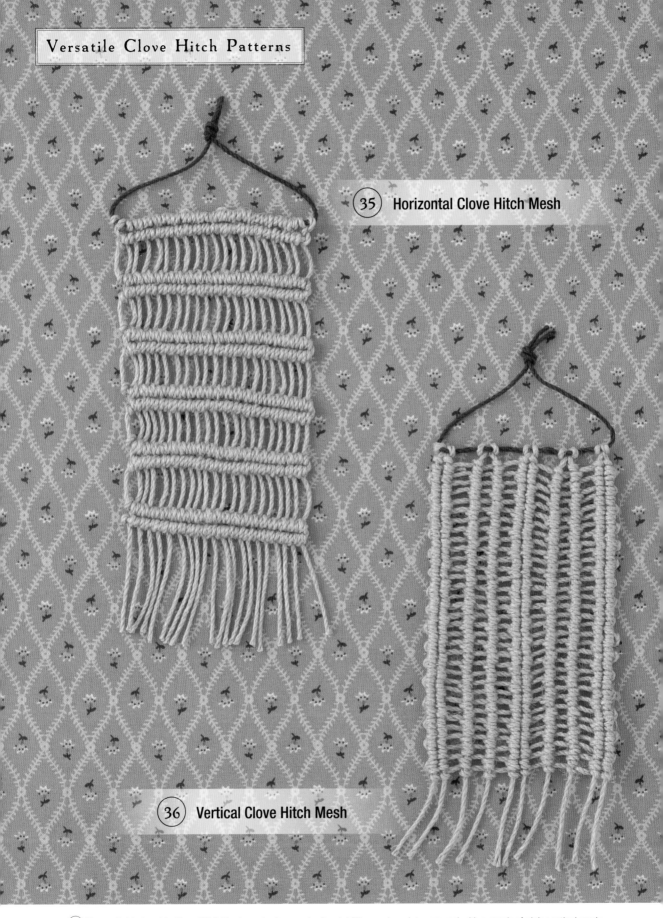

(35) Horizontal Clove Hitch Mesh

(36) Vertical Clove Hitch Mesh

(35) Rows of side-by-side Clove Hitch Knots worked over a horizontal filler cord are interspersed with a mesh of plain vertical cords.

(36) Here the knots are worked over vertical filler cords; the mesh is created by the working cord as it travels across the panel.

37 **Reverse Clove Hitch Texture**

38 **Clove Hitch Striped Texture**

37 The "wrong" side of the Clove Hitch makes an interesting pattern too, especially when worked to cross in 2 directions.

38 This ribbed texture is made of alternating rows of Horizontal Clove Hitch and Reverse Clove Hitch Knots.

K n o t K n o w - h o w
Clove Hitch Knots

The Clove Hitch is also known as a Double Half Hitch Knot. The loops of this knot can be aligned horizontally, vertically, diagonally, and in a fourth variation, in "reverse." The wrapping of the knot itself is essentially the same for all, and each can be wrapped from left-to-right or right-to-left. In the symbols, the line that breaks next to the center dot indicates the working (tying) cord. The terms are confusing, so just follow the directions to learn each version.

 ## Horizontal Clove Hitch

Here multiple working cords are individually tied over a single filler cord, which bends back and forth across the work to support each subsequent row of knots. Each knot makes 2 loops, side-by-side over the horizontal filler cord.

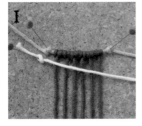

1 Attach vertical cords to an anchor cord. Pin a horizontal filler cord at the left edge as shown.

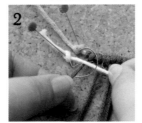

2 Hold the filler cord in your right hand. Follow the arrow to wrap the vertical cord at the left edge over the filler cord.

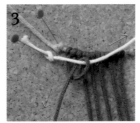

3 Lift the filler cord slightly and gently pull the vertical cord tight.

4 Half the Clove Hitch is complete.

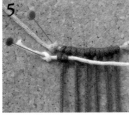

5 Repeat steps 2 and 3 with the same vertical cord, being sure to pass it from back to front through the horizontal loop it makes below the anchor cord. Now, working from left to right, repeat steps 2, 3, and 5 with each remaining vertical cord.

6 At the end of the row, fold the filler cord across the work as shown and pin it down at the fold. Follow the arrow to make the first half Clove Hitch with the vertical cord at the right edge, (wrapping opposite to the direction of the first row).

7 Repeat step 6 with the same cord, passing it from back to front through the horizontal loop it makes below the anchor cord; pull tightly.

8 One Clove Hitch is complete at the right end of the second row. Working from right to left, repeat the knotting as in steps 6–7 with each remaining vertical cord.

 ## Vertical Clove Hitch

Here a single working cord is knotted across a set of vertical filler cords, reversing direction at the end of each row. Each knot makes a stack of 2 loops over its vertical filler cord.

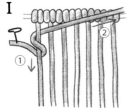

1 Attach vertical filler cords to an anchor cord. Pin a working cord at the left edge and wrap it around the first filler cord as shown.

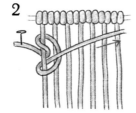

2 Wrap the working cord around the same filler cord again, being sure to pass it from back to front through the vertical loop it forms as shown. Pull to tighten.

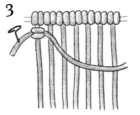

3 One vertical Clove Hitch is complete.

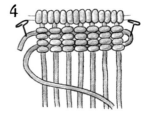

4 Tie a Clove Hitch as in steps 1–2 on each subsequent filler cord. At the end of the row, fold the working cord over; pin the fold. Work another row from right to left, wrapping in the opposite direction.

Diagonal Clove Hitch
A variation of the Horizontal Clove Hitch.

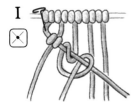

1 Use the first vertical cord as the filler cord. Make Horizontal Clove Hitches over it as shown, tying each slightly below (or above) its neighbor so a diagonal ridge forms.

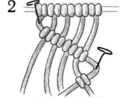

2 At the end of the row, bend the filler cord as shown. To reverse the direction in which the loops slant, reverse the direction in which you wrap the working cord.

Reverse Clove Hitch
Here the "back" of the knot shows on the front.

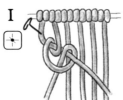

1 Use the first vertical cord as the filler cord. Follow the drawing to knot the second vertical cord over it (wrapping first over and around, then under and around).

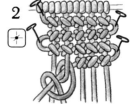

2 Knot alternate rows in the reverse direction (as shown above) to make the top "bar" of the knots slant opposite to those of the previous row.

(35) Horizontal Clove Hitch Mesh

Leave an open space after every 2 rows of Horizontal Clove Hitches, letting the filler cord float down at the edge before bending it back.

photo page **64**

🌼 **Knotting Diagram**   ← Attach the filler cord.

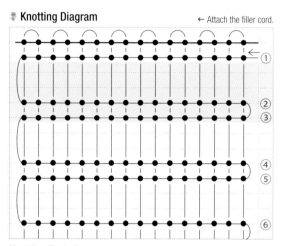

Knotting Technique

 Horizontal Clove Hitch → page 66

(36) Vertical Clove Hitch Mesh

Set up the vertical cords in pairs, spacing them as shown. The greater the interval between pairs, the wider the open part of the mesh.

photo page **64**

🌼 **Knotting Diagram**   → Attach the filler cord.

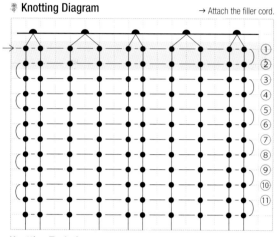

Knotting Technique

 Vertical Clove Hitch → page 66

(37) Reverse Clove Hitch Texture

The crossed cords of Reverse Clove Hitch Knots worked in horizontal rows create a sideways herringbone texture.

photo page **65**

🌼 **Knotting Diagram**   ← Attach the filler cord.

Knotting Technique

 Reverse Clove Hitch → page 66

(38) Clove Hitch Striped Texture

This ribbed texture resembles an ottoman fabric; it is made of alternating rows of Horizontal Clove Hitch and Reverse Clove Hitch knots.

photo page **65**

🌼 **Knotting Diagram**   → Attach the filler cord.

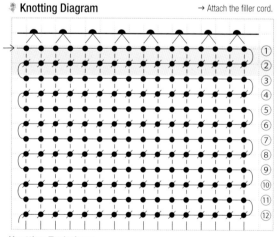

Knotting Technique

 Horizontal Clove Hitch → page 66   Reverse Clove Hitch → page 66

39 Clove Hitch Checkerboard Mesh

40 Horizontal Clove Hitch with Twisted Mesh

39 Solid squares of Vertical and Horizontal Clove Hitch Knots alternate with a mesh of vertical cords.

40 A simple mesh made of crisscrossed vertical cords alternates with single rows of Vertical Clove Hitches.

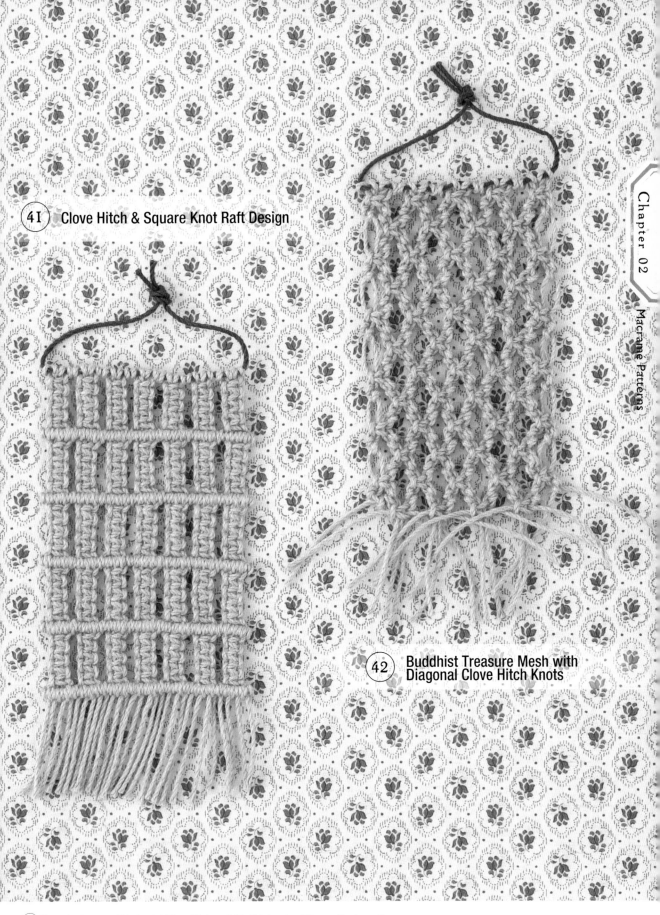

41 Clove Hitch & Square Knot Raft Design

42 Buddhist Treasure Mesh with Diagonal Clove Hitch Knots

41 Here single rows of Horizontal Clove Hitches divide tidy bands of Square Knot sennits.

42 Diagonal Clove Hitches make a pretty addition to panel design ㉓, a basic Buddhist Treasure Mesh.

(39) Clove Hitch Checkerboard Mesh

The solid squares of this design include both Horizontal and Vertical Clove Hitches. Check often to see that the open and knotted sections are equal in size.

photo page 68

✿ Knotting Diagram
→ Attach the filler cord.

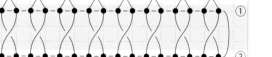

Knotting Technique

Vertical Clove Hitch
→ page 66

Horizontal Clove Hitch
→ page 66

Instructions

1

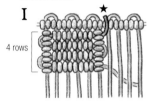

4 rows

For rows 1–4, attach a cord at the spot marked ★ (for each solid square) and use it as working cord or filler cord as needed to work the knots shown in the diagram.

2

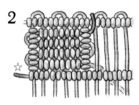

For row 5, attach a filler cord at the spot marked ☆ and work Horizontal Clove Hitches all the way across.

3 Pass ★ cord to the back and down

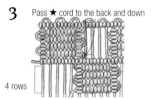

4 rows

Pass each cord marked ★ behind the knots in row 5 and, beginning at the left edge, work rows 6–9 of the next (offset) squares.

4

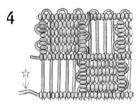

Pass the ☆ cord down along the right edge of the work and use it as the filler cord for row 10. Repeat rows 1–10 until the panel is the desired length.

---

(40) Horizontal Clove Hitch with Twisted Mesh

To make the mesh, after working each row of knots, give each pair of vertical cords a half twist – so the left becomes the right.

photo page 68

✿ Knotting Diagram
→ Attach the filler cord.

Knotting Technique

Vertical Clove Hitch → page 66

Instructions

1

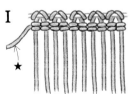

Attach the working cord ★ at the left edge and then make 1 row of Vertical Clove Hitch Knots.

2

Lift first cord.

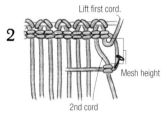

Mesh height

2nd cord

Lift the first vertical cord out of the way. Bring the working cord down; leave a gap the height of the mesh and make a Vertical Clove Hitch on the second vertical cord.

3

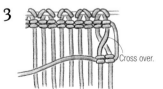

Cross over.

Bring the first vertical cord down again and cross it over the cord with the knot; then make another knot on it.

4

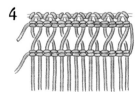

In this manner, cross each pair of cords as you knot the rest of the row. Repeat steps 2–4 until the panel is the desired length.

41 Clove Hitch & Square Knot Raft Design

Here 4-row Square Knot sennits alternate with a single row of Horizontal Clove Hitch knots to make a geometric, tailored mesh.

photo page 69

🌿 Knotting Diagram

→ Attach the filler cord.

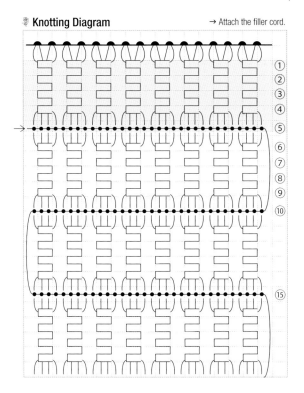

Knotting Technique

 Left-facing Square Knot → page 31

 Horizontal Clove Hitch → page 66

Tip

Plan the cord length correctly

The base of this design is the Square Knot sennits, which each is worked with a group of 4 vertical cords. In each group, the outer 2 are the working cords and should be 4 times the length of the inner 2 filler cords over which they are tied. The Clove Hitches are worked over an added filler cord.

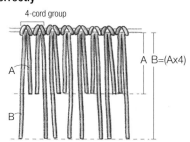

4-cord group

A B=(Ax4)

A

B

---

42 Buddhist Treasure Mesh with Diagonal Clove Hitch Knots

This variation of the basic Buddhist Treasure Mesh ㉓ features a Diagonal Clove Hitch tied on the cords linking the offset Square Knots.

photo page 69

🌿 Knotting Diagram

Knotting Technique

 Left-facing Square Knot → page 31

 Diagonal Clove Hitch → page 66

Instructions

1

For row 1, make a Square Knot on each group of 4 vertical cords.

2

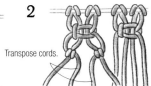

Transpose cords.

For row 2, take the 2 cords that served as filler cords in the Square Knot and tie each to the working cord at its right or left using a Diagonal Clove Hitch. Repeat across.

3

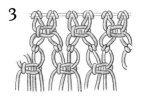

For row 3, skip the 2 cords at the left edge and then make a Square Knot with each subsequent group of 4 vertical cords.

4

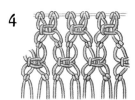

For row 4, repeat row 2. Repeat rows 1–4 until the panel is the desired length.

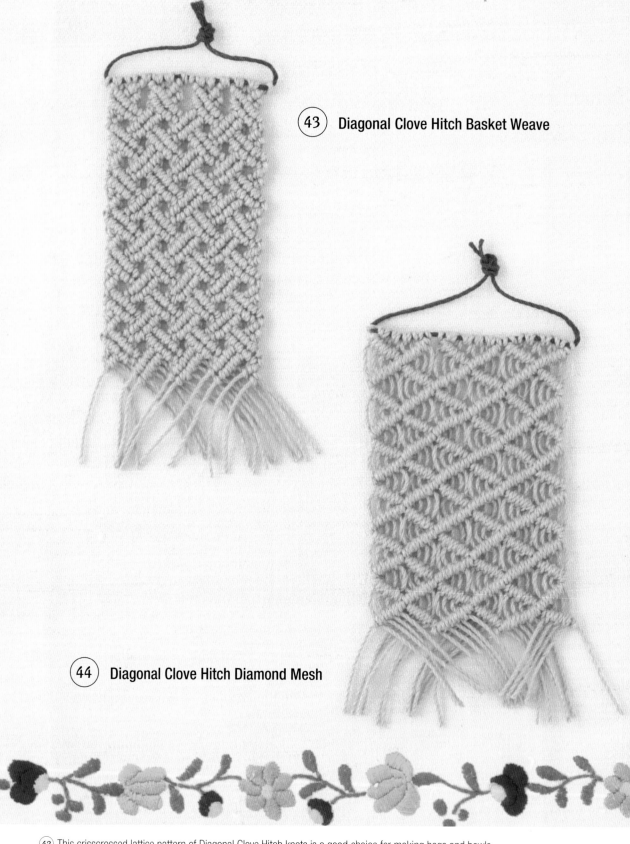

43 Diagonal Clove Hitch Basket Weave

44 Diagonal Clove Hitch Diamond Mesh

43 This crisscrossed lattice pattern of Diagonal Clove Hitch knots is a good choice for making bags and bowls.

44 An open-mesh diamond pattern that can be subtly changed if you tie the knots at a steeper angle.

(45) **Diagonal Clove Hitch Wood Grain Mesh**

(46) **Diagonal Clove Hitch Eyelet Diamond Mesh**

(45) This pattern is reminiscent of Celtic knitting motifs and cross-stitch designs found Northern and Eastern Europe.

(46) These diamonds are filled with basic Buddhist Treasure Mesh ㉓ and outlined with Diagonal Clove Hitch Knots.

43 Diagonal Clove Hitch Basket Weave

Look carefully at the symbols to see how the cords travel and the knot wrapping direction changes (left-to-right or right-to-left) to create this 6-cord, 6-row pattern.

photo page 72

Knotting Diagram

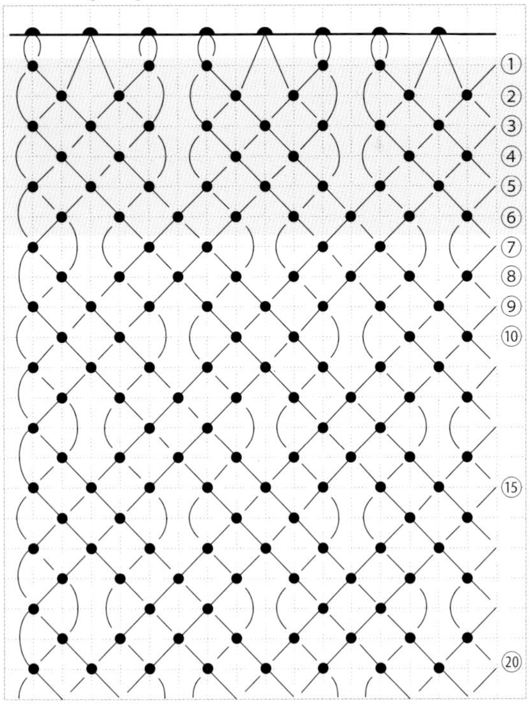

Knotting Technique

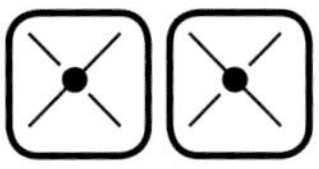

Diagonal Clove Hitch → page 66

Tip

Plan the cord length correctly

The foundation of this pattern is the X pattern that is formed by knotting 6 rows of 6 cords. In each group, the 2 middle cords are the working cords (B in the drawing at right), and they have to be about 1¾ times the length of the filler cords (A).

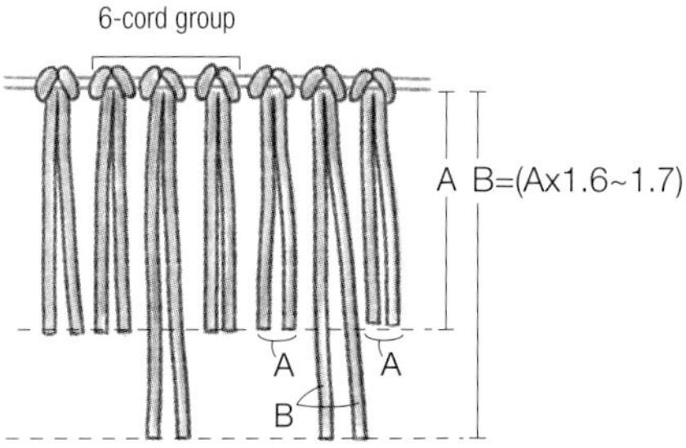

44 Diagonal Clove Hitch Diamond Mesh

Look carefully at the photo and symbols and keep your knots moving at a consistent angle to create this 10-cord, 10-row horizontal diamond pattern.

photo page 72

Knotting Diagram

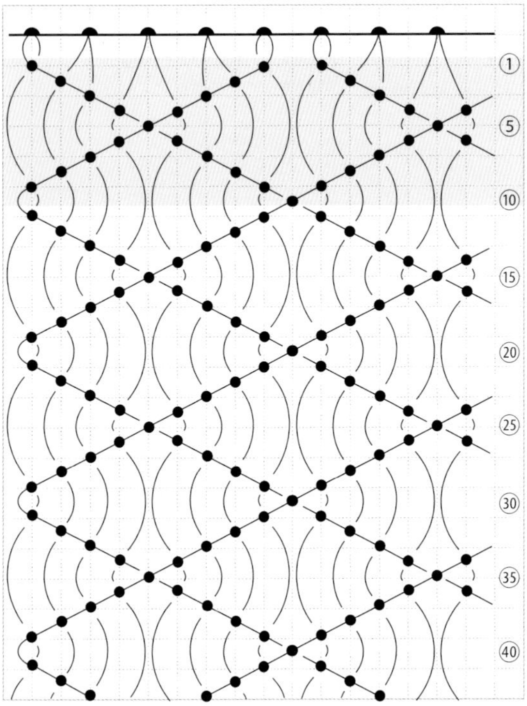

Knotting Technique

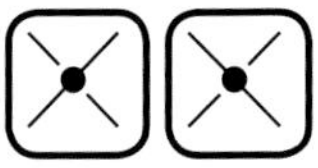

Diagonal Clove Hitch → page 66

Tip

Join the points correctly

Every time you reach the place where the diagonal lines cross to enclose the diamond shape, knot the left filler cord onto the right one as shown. By doing this, you will create a line that neatly progresses downward from the upper right to the lower left.

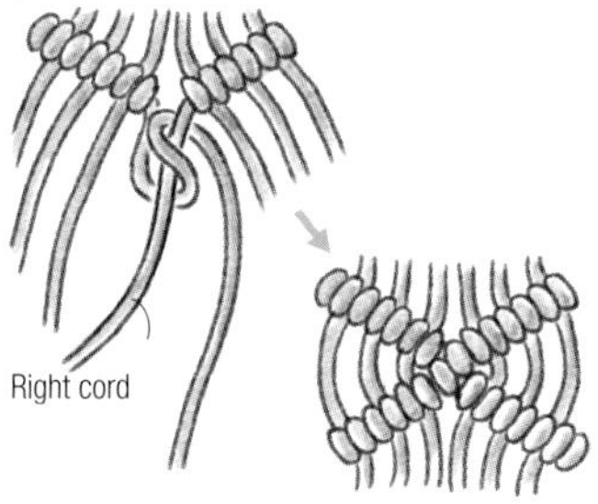

(45) Diagonal Clove Hitch Wood Grain Mesh

Because the pattern of intersecting points is staggered in this 10-cord, 8-row design, it is important to pull the intersections tight.

photo page 73

🧵 Knotting Diagram

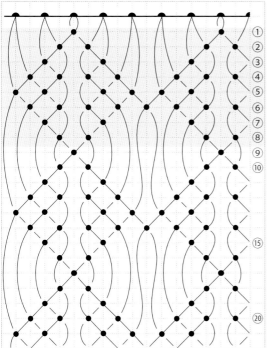

① ② ③ ④ ⑤ ⑥ ⑦ ⑧ ⑨ ⑩ ⑮ ⑳

Knotting Technique

Left-facing Square Knot → page 31

Tip

Plan the cord length correctly

There are 10 cords meandering in each section of this design. The rule of thumb for planning their length? Cut each cord to be 10 times the desired length of your panel (20 times the length if beginning with 5 doubled cords). You will end up with cords of different lengths, but it's best to estimate about 10 times the length.

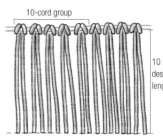

10-cord group

10 x the desired length

(46) Diagonal Clove Hitch Eyelet Diamond Mesh

These diamonds are filled with the basic Buddhist Treasure Mesh. The best way to work this 12-cord, 14-row pattern is to knot the mesh first, and then work the Clove Hitch outlines.

photo page 73

🧵 Knotting Diagram

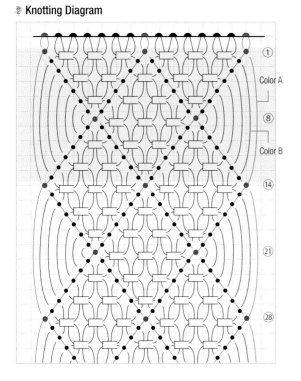

① Color A ⑧ Color B ⑭ ㉑ ㉘

Knotting Technique

Left-facing Square Knot → page 31

Diagonal Clove Hitch → page 66

Tip

Figure the right number of cords

You need 14 vertical cords to create 1 diamond motif; however, to balance the pattern, you need an extra cord at each end of your panel. To plan the total needed, decide how many diamonds across you want (the knotting diagram shows 2), multiply by 14, and add 2. We made the sample with 12 cords of 1 color between 2 cords of a contrast color, plus 1 additional contrast cord at each edge.

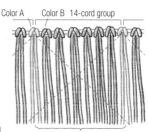

Color A Color B 14-cord group

Cords used to create 1 diamond

(47) Diagonal Clove Hitch Chevron Pattern

(48) Diagonal Clove Hitch Serpentine Mesh

(47) This chevron pattern is dense and firm, reminiscent of a knitting pattern. Lots of knots!

(48) This mesh features nesting, overlapping serpentine lines that travel back and forth in a regular, and very simple, pattern.

49 Diagonal Clove Hitch Floret Mesh

50 Diagonal Clove Hitch Daisy Mesh

49 A sweet mesh with pairs of eyelets offset in alternate rows. Thread a ribbon between through the longer openings if you like.

50 The daisy-like motif in this mesh is linked by Square Knots; the pattern resembles an embroidered eyelet fabric.

47 · Diagonal Clove Hitch Chevron Pattern

This is a firm, dense fabric. Each chevron requires 12 vertical cords (the photo shows 2 chevrons, the knotting diagram 1½ chevrons).

photo page 76

⚜ Knotting Diagram

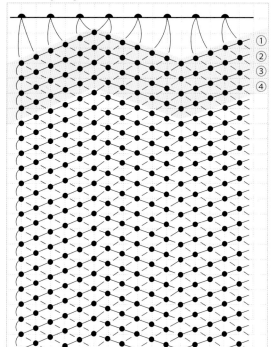

Knotting Technique

Diagonal Clove Hitch → page 66

 Tip

Fill in the zigzag ends if you like

Because this pattern is made up entirely of Diagonal Clove Hitches, the ends of the panel have a zigzag contour. If you prefer to make the ends straight, add knots to the top and bottom very carefully—so as not to distort the angles of the herringbone pattern—as shown in pink at right.

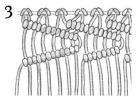

Top

Bottom

---

48 · Diagonal Clove Hitch Serpentine Mesh

Look carefully at the diagram to see how the curving lines of knots overlap and nest—you must begin the highest end of each line before finishing the lowest end of the line below it.

photo page 76

⚜ Knotting Diagram

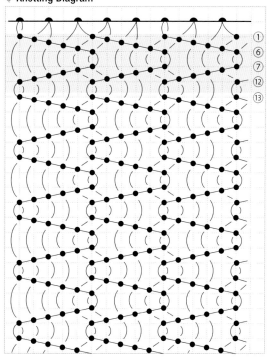

① ⑥ ⑦ ⑫ ⑬

Knotting Technique

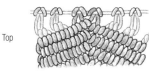
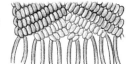

Diagonal Clove Hitch → page 66

Instructions

1

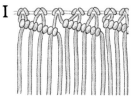

Set up a multiple of 6 vertical cords. Beginning at the left edge, make 4 Diagonal Clove Hitch knots with every 5 cords as shown; end with 6 knots at the right edge.

2

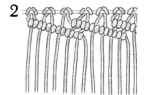

Work 2 more knots at the right end of each line of 4 knots, as shown.

3

Bend the each filler cord back to the left and make the first 4 knots of the second line; end with 6 knots at the left edge.

4

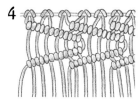

Work 2 more knots at the left end of each line of 4 knots, as shown. Repeat the knotting sequence in steps 1–4 until the panel is the desired length.

(49) Diagonal Clove Hitch Floret Mesh

A sweet mesh of interlaced, offset eyelets, this is an 8-cord, 10-row pattern.

photo page 77

Knotting Diagram

③
④
⑤
⑥
⑦
⑧
⑨
⑩

Knotting Technique

Diagonal Clove Hitch → page 66

Tip

Border the edges correctly

You can see from the Knotting Diagram (at left) that on the left edge of the panel, the first 2 cords of this pattern must be treated differently on rows 7 and 10 in order to finish the design in a neat and balanced way where it's not possible to continue the crisscrossing lines. Do the same thing on the right edge of your panel. The outlined section ⓐ on the right shows how this works on 8 cords, the fewest you can use for this pattern.

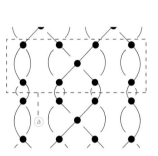

ⓐ

---

(50) Diagonal Clove Hitch Daisy Mesh

These round motifs are linked by Square Knots, and a Square Knot sits at the center of each as well. This is a 6-cord, 5-row pattern, but note that row 1 is different—repeat rows 2–6.

photo page 77

Knotting Diagram

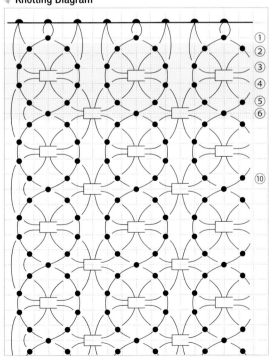

③
④
⑤
⑥

⑩

Knotting Technique

Left-facing Square Knot → page 31

Diagonal Clove Hitch → page 66

Instructions

1

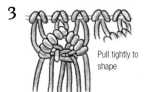

6-cord group

Set up your work with a multiple of 6 vertical cords.

2

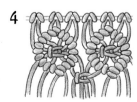

Follow the Knotting Diagram to make the Diagonal Clove Hitches in rows 1–3 (row 1 uses the 2 middle cords of each group).

3

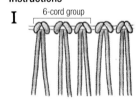

Pull tightly to shape

Complete row 3 by making a Square Knot with the 4 cords in the middle of each group. Adjust so the Clove Hitches make a semicircle.

4

Follow the Knotting Diagram to work rows 4–6, making the Square Knots after completing all the Clove Hitches. Repeat rows 2–6 until the panel is the desired length.

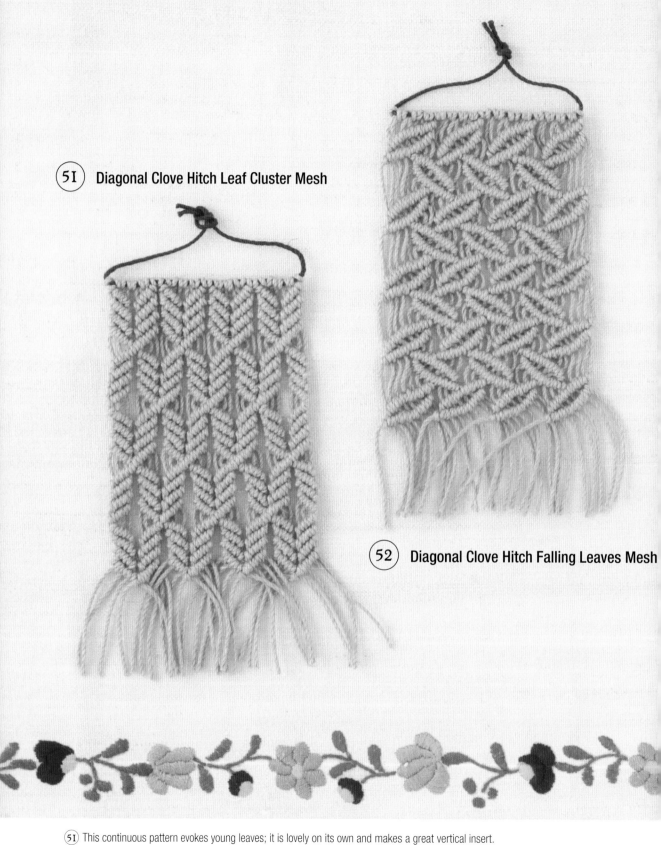

(51) Diagonal Clove Hitch Leaf Cluster Mesh

(52) Diagonal Clove Hitch Falling Leaves Mesh

(51) This continuous pattern evokes young leaves; it is lovely on its own and makes a great vertical insert.

(52) A simple overall texture. For fun, try it with assorted cord colors to evoke a cascade of autumn leaves.

54 Diagonal Clove Hitch Lily Flower Mesh

53 Diagonal Clove Hitch Leaf-and-Bud Mesh

㊾ Small leaf clusters become small flowers when a Square Knot Bump is worked at the center of the motif.

㊻ A simple 4-petal flower motif that makes an interesting, bold overall mesh when repeated.

51 Diagonal Clove Hitch Leaf Cluster Mesh

Because there are very few points of intersection in this pattern, you can add beads in some of the empty areas to enhance the design and add strength. One sequence is complete in 20 rows.

photo page 80

Knotting Diagram

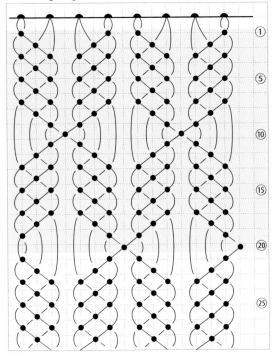

Knotting Technique

  Diagonal Clove Hitch → page 66

Tip

Work with a multiple of 4 cords

To see the full pattern you need to begin with at least 16 vertical cords. However, the design is based on a 4-cord pattern that reverses back and forth across the work, and you can use any multiple of 4 that gives you the width you want. Look at the left edge of row 20 to see how to handle a narrow repeat.

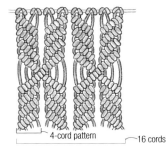

4-cord pattern   16 cords

---

52 Diagonal Clove Hitch Falling Leaves Mesh

Set up your work with a multiple of 16 vertical cords, using at least 32 to see the full pattern; then follow the Knotting Diagram.

photo page 80

Knotting Diagram

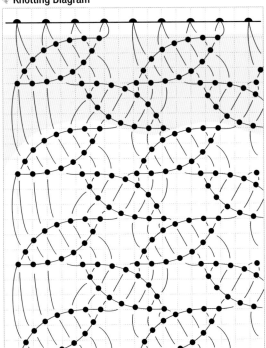

Knotting Technique

  Diagonal Clove Hitch → page 66

Tip

Only the leaf tips touch the edges

Because the leaf motifs in this design are reversed on every other vertical repeat, the edges of the panel are mostly long, unknotted "floating" sections of cord. Keep an eye on your tension to see that the edges neither bind nor droop.

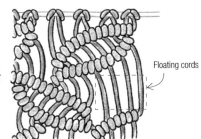

Floating cords

(53) Diagonal Clove Hitch Leaf-and-Bud Mesh

This is a variation of (51) Leaf Cluster Mesh. You can add a little bud where the leaves intersect by making a 3-knot Bump (14).

photo page 81

❀ Knotting Diagram

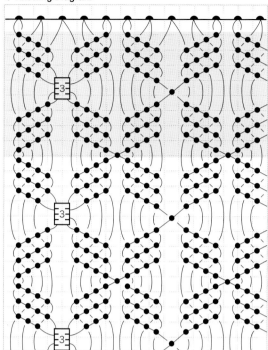

Knotting Technique

 Knotted-Loop Bump → page 42

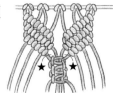 Diagonal Clove Hitch → page 66

Instructions (for leaflets with bud)

I

Using 8 vertical cords, knot 3 rows of Diagonal Clove Hitches, and then with the middle 4 cords, make 3 Square Knots.

2

Insert the 2 filler cords from the Square Knots from front to back through the holes marked ★ in step 1. Pull tight and make another Square Knot.

3

Use the 2 filler cords from the Square Knots as the anchor cords for the next row of Diagonal Clove Hitches.

4

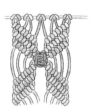

Three rows of Diagonal Clove Hitches below the Square Knot bud complete the motif.

---

(54) Diagonal Clove Hitch Lily Flower Mesh

Here an overall pattern of simple blossoms with raised centers makes a bold, graphic mesh. Keep the petal contours regular.

photo page 81

❀ Knotting Diagram

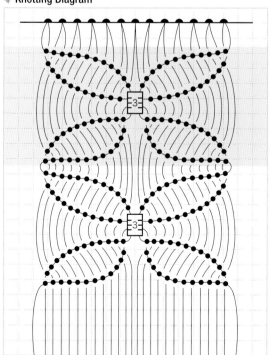

Knotting Technique

Knotted-Loop Bump → page 42

Diagonal Clove Hitch → page 66

Tip

Customize your blooms

The width of the flowers depends on the number of cords. The Knotting Diagram and photo on page 81 show a blossom wider than it is tall, worked with 26 vertical cords. At right the pattern is worked with only 14 cords, making the motif squarer. Experiment to see how you can change this design.

(56) **Nut Lattice**

(55) **Macadamia Dots**

(55) This mesh of 3-knot Bumps has a heavily textured yet even surface — great for mats or baskets.

(56) The arresting feature of this lattice pattern is the ribbed balls that look a bit like walnuts in their shells.

(57) Falling Nuts Mesh

(58) Flower and Nut Mesh

(57) A pretty and rather intricate pattern, with dimensional "nuts" set into a basic Buddhist Treasure Mesh.

(58) This charming mix of flower and the nut motifs is appropriate for bags and pouches.

Macadamia Dots

This is a heavily textured variation of the Buddhist Treasure Mesh ㉓:
After the first row, make a 3-knot Bump ⑭ at every intersection.

Knotting Diagram

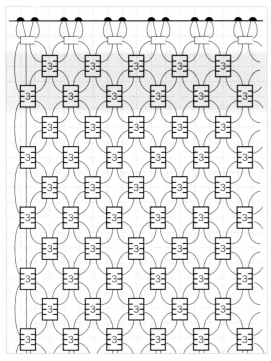

Knotting Technique

 Knotted-Loop Bump
→ page 42

 Left-facing Square Knot
→ page 31

Instructions

I

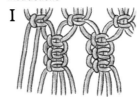

Follow the Knotting Diagram to make 1 row of Square Knots. Work all subsequent rows with 3-knot Bumps: To begin each row, make 3 Square Knots at each position.

2

Insert the 2 filler cords from the Square Knots from front to back through the holes marked ★.

3

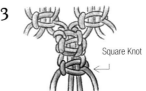

Square Knot ←

Pull tight and make another Square Knot.

4

The Bump is complete. Repeat across. Repeat as shown, offsetting the knot positions on subsequent rows.

Nut Lattice

A 20-cord, 10-row pattern of diagonals alternating with ribbed "nuts" and little starbursts made of Square Knots tied over 6 filler cords.

Knotting Diagram

Knotting Technique

Square Knot
→ page 31

Diagonal Clove Hitch
→ page 66

Instructions (for ribbed nuts)

I

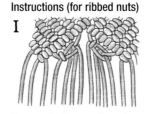

Complete the Diagonal Clove Hitch half-diamonds as shown. Make a Square Knot on each edge of this shape (use the top 4 cords); pull tight.

2

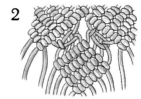

Using the cords of the right-hand Square Knot as filler cords, work 4 rows of Diagonal Clove Hitches as shown.

3

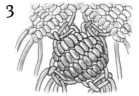

Make a Square Knot on each edge of this shape as shown. Pull the knots tight to make the "nut" round upward.

4

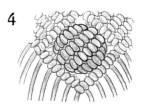

Add a border of Diagonal Clove Hitches to complete the pattern and begin the next diamonds.

(57) Falling Nuts Mesh

Here a nut shape is interspersed with lozenges of Buddhist Treasure Mesh bordered by Diagonal Clove Hitch "leaves." It's complicated — make a full diagram if you want to make a wider fabric.

photo page 85

❃ Knotting Diagram

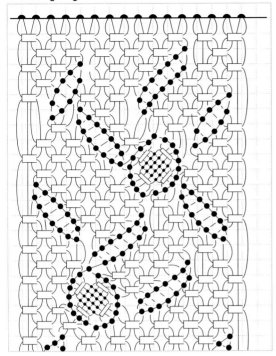

Knotting Technique

 Square Knot → page 31

  Diagonal Clove Hitch → page 66

Instructions (for ribbed nuts)

1

Follow the Knotting Diagram until you've made the top of a nut enclosure with 5 Diagonal Clove Hitches on the left and 4 on the right.

2

Referring to steps 1–3 of (56) on the opposite page, make the nut shape.

3

Add a border of Diagonal Clove Hitches along the bottom of the nut.

4

To close the border, use the right filler cord to tie a Clove Hitch around the left filler cord. Now fill in and continue the mesh pattern.

---

(58) Flower and Nut Mesh

A tessellated design of interlocking flowers and nuts. At the center of each blossom is a 3-knot Knotted-Loop Bump. Begin with a row of Square Knots → p. 31.

photo page 85

❃ Knotting Diagram

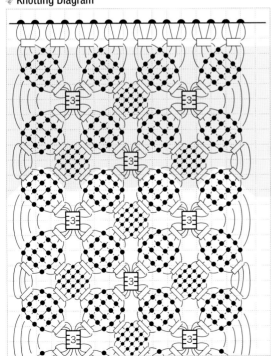

Knotting Technique

 Knotted-Loop Bumps → page 42

  Diagonal Clove Hitch → page 66

Instructions

1

Follow the Knotting Diagram to make the top row of petal shapes, ending each with a Square Knot.

2

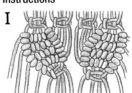

Join the petals in pairs as shown, making a Bump of Square Knots that have 6 filler cords.

3

Make the nut shape with the 8 cords hanging between the joined flowers by following steps 2–3 of (56) on the opposite page.

4

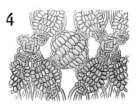

Follow the Knotting Diagram to make the next row of petal shapes, ending each with a Square Knot.

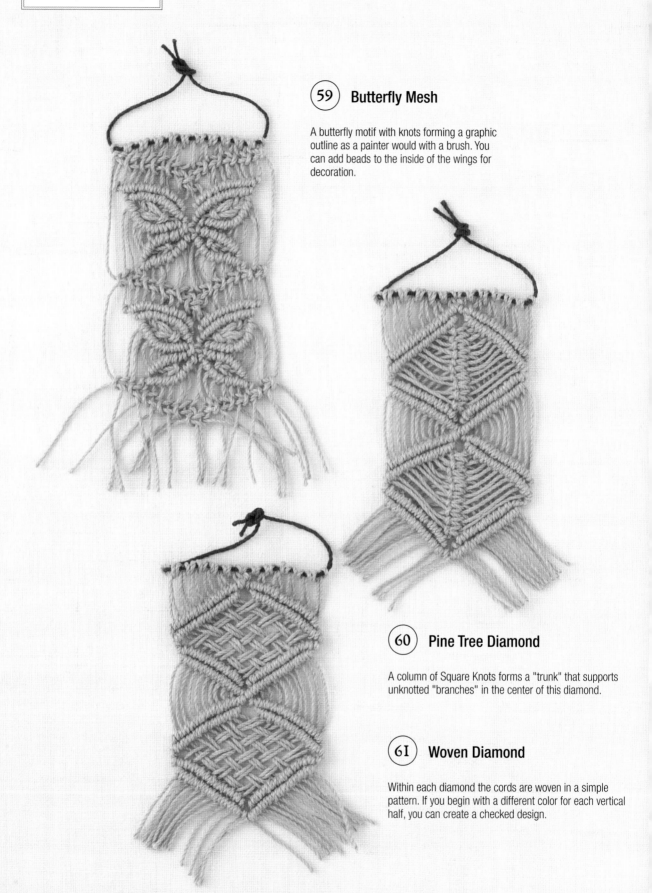

(59) Butterfly Mesh

A butterfly motif with knots forming a graphic outline as a painter would with a brush. You can add beads to the inside of the wings for decoration.

(60) Pine Tree Diamond

A column of Square Knots forms a "trunk" that supports unknotted "branches" in the center of this diamond.

(61) Woven Diamond

Within each diamond the cords are woven in a simple pattern. If you begin with a different color for each vertical half, you can create a checked design.

⑥ Mossy Diamond

The dense Clove Hitch filling of this diamond has the look of a thick carpet or a knitter's Moss Stitch.

⑥ Awaji Knot Diamond

A nice use of decorative knots at the corners and in the center makes this motif especially distinctive. It's not difficult to make.

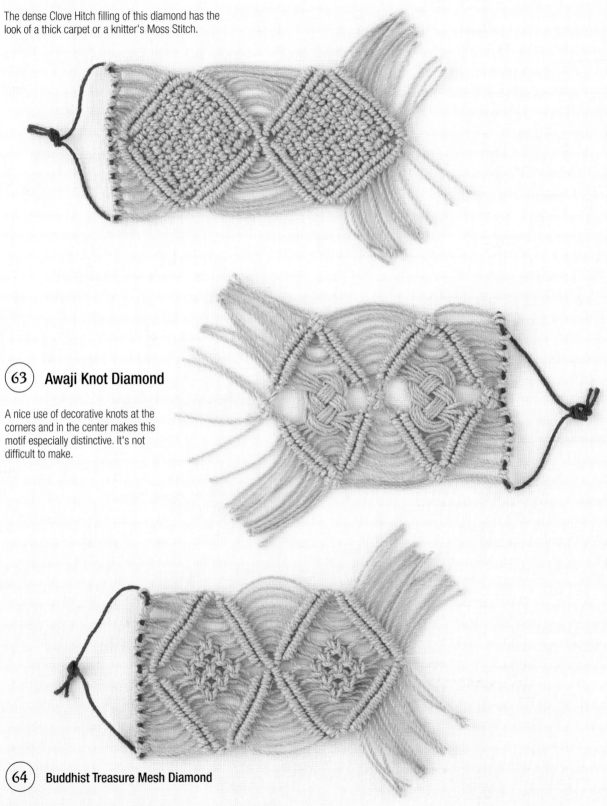

⑥ Buddhist Treasure Mesh Diamond

The cluster of offset Square Knots in the middle of this diamond is a fragment of Buddhist Treasure Mesh ㉓ Use it as a simple, easy accent.

(59) Butterfly Mesh

Each butterfly motif requires 20 vertical cords; add 1 cord at each end or 2 in between motifs to balance the design. Keep the shapes consistent.

photo page 88

Knotting Diagram

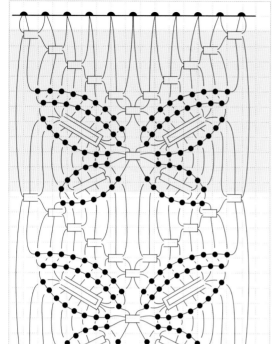

Knotting Technique

 Square Knot → page 31

 Diagonal Clove Hitch → page 66

Instructions

1
Follow the Knotting Diagram to make the Square Knot background and then the top edge of the top wings (2 rows of Diagonal Clove Hitches).

2
In the center of each wing make an extra-large 8-cord Square Knot (4 cords for the filler, tied with 2 cords held together on each side); leave these loose so they lie flat.

3
Complete the lower edge of the top wings.

4
Using the 4 cords at the middle of the work, make 1 Left-Facing Square Knot to connect the wings.

5
Continue as shown on the Knotting Diagram; make a Square Knot with 4 cords in the middle of each bottom wing, keeping it loose so it lies flat.

6
Complete the lower edge of the bottom wings. Repeat steps 1–6 until the panel is the desired length.

---

(60) Pine Tree Diamond

Work the top outline of the diamond first. Then make the central Square Knot column, placing the working cords behind after tying. Then complete the diamond outline.

photo page 88

Knotting Diagram

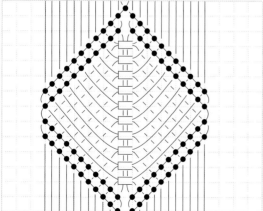

Knotting Technique

 Diagonal Clove Hitch → page 66

 Square Knot → page 31

---

(61) Woven Diamond

Work the top outline of the diamond first. Then weave the center — 2 cords at a time, over and under. Then complete the diamond outline.

photo page 88

Knotting Diagram

Knotting Technique

  Diagonal Clove Hitch → page 66

(63) Awaji Knot Diamond

First knot the 4 middle cords. Then work the top outline of the diamond; then the Awaji Knot (use 4 cords as one); then the corner knots. Work the bottom outline last.

photo page 89

🌿 Knotting Diagram

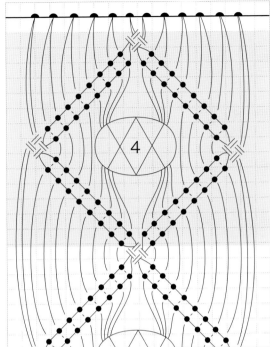

Knotting Technique

 4-ply Round Lanyard → below

 page 66

 page 47

Instructions (to begin the design)

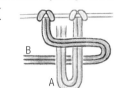

1 Use each of the center pairs of cords as 1 cord. First fold cord A as shown; then fold cord B around it.

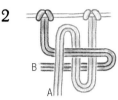

2 Fold cord A down over cord B.

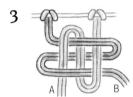

3 Fold cord B over and pass its end through the bottom loop made by cord A.

4 Pull the ends of the cords to tighten the knot.

---

(62) Mossy Diamond

Look carefully at the photo and Knotting Diagram to see how to change each cord from filler to working cord so the knots slant in groups of four.

photo page 89

🌿 Knotting Diagram

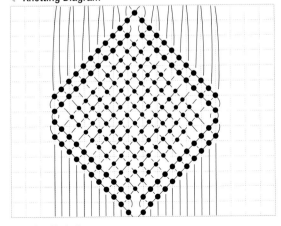

Knotting Technique

  Diagonal Clove Hitch → page 66

---

(64) Buddhist Treasure Mesh Diamond

Work the top outline of the diamond first. Then work Square Knots in the center as shown. Then complete the diamond outline.

photo page 89

🌿 Knotting Diagram

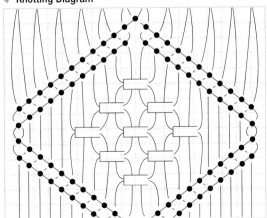

Knotting Technique

  Diagonal Clove Hitch → page 66

 Square Knot → page 31

91

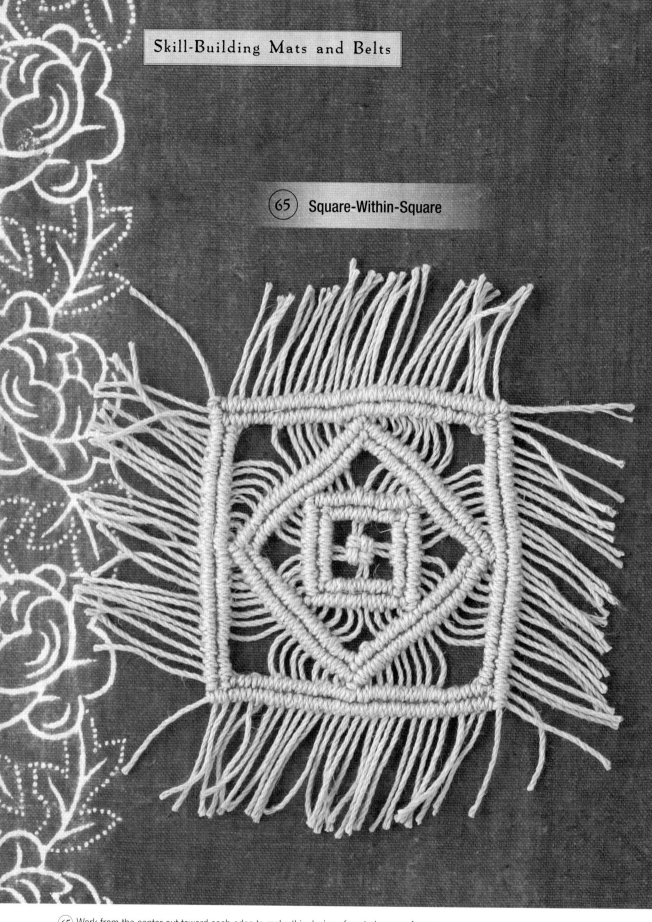

65 Square-Within-Square

65 Work from the center out toward each edge to make this design of nested square frames.

66 It's intriguing to see how the concentric rings of this flower-like pattern build out from the center.

66 Circular Flower

67 Lark's Head Knot Lace Band

68 Square Knot Braided Band

67 Small picots add to the lacy effect of this narrow band. Jazz it up by stringing on some beads.

68 This band of interlocked pieces is very simple to knot – use it as a belt, bracelet, or headband.

(65) Square-Within-Square

Begin with a single 4-ply Round Lanyard Knot ⑰ at the center of the piece; then work out, adding filler cords and working cords along the way.

photo page 92

⚜ Knotting Diagram

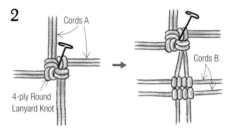

Knotting Technique

Horizontal Clove Hitch → page 66	4-ply Round Lanyard → page 66

Instructions

*for soft jute cord (2mm)

	Location	*Length (each)	Cords needed
A	Center knot	28"/70cm	4
B	Row 1 filler cords	28"/70cm	8
C	Row 1 vertical cords	28"/70cm	8
D	Row 2 filler cords	22"/55cm	8
E	Row 2 vertical cords	20"/50cm	8
F	Row 3 filler cords	14"/35cm	8
G	Row 3 vertical cords	14"/35cm	12

1 The sample in the photo is made of jute cord and measures 4"/10cm square. The length of cord required will vary with its weight, but the table above can be a guide.

2

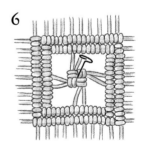

To begin, using 2 cords together as 1, tie a single Round Lanyard knot (⑰ steps 1–6 on p. 43). Pin the knot to the board. Center 2 B cords across 1 pair of A cords and tie them together using Horizontal Clove Hitches as shown.

3

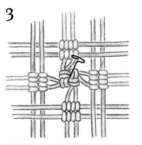

Add 2 B cords to each remaining pair of A cords

4

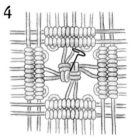

Attach the 8 C cords, folding each in half (in pink, next to the A cords).

5

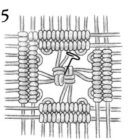

Finish 1 corner of the square, tying Horizontal Clove Hitches as shown in pink.

6

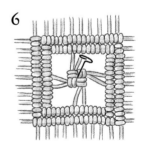

Finish the other corners the same way; tighten the knots and arrange into a neat square shape.

7 Continue in this manner, adding first the diamond-shape frame and then the outer square frame. Always affix the filler cords at their midpoint first; then work out to each corner. Trim the ends of the cords to form a neat fringe.

(67) Lark's Head Knot Lace Band

As you work, keep the sections parallel to one another; to join the outer section to the inner, twist the working cords when you make the small picots between rows 5 and 6.

photo page 93

⚜ Knotting Diagram

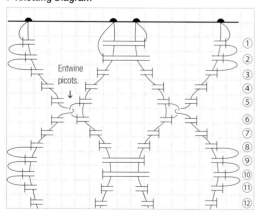

Entwine picots.

①
②
③
④
⑤
⑥
⑦
⑧
⑨
⑩
⑪
⑫

Knotting Technique

Vertical Lark's Head Knot → page 35

(66) Circular Flower

The shaping and attaching of the "petals" on the concentric bands of this flower is clever: the filler cord loops back and forth, held in place with knots.

photo page 93

❧ Knotting Diagram

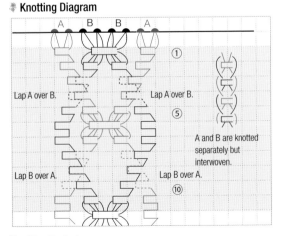

Knotting Technique

 Vertical Lark's Head Knot→ page 66

 Horizontal Clove Hitch → page 66

Instructions

*for soft jute cord (2mm)

	Location	*Length (each)	Cords needed
A	Central filler cord	10"/25cm	1
B	Row 1 (inner petals) filler cord	24"/60cm	1
C	Row 1 working cord	24"/60cm	2
D	Row 2 (middle petals) filler cord	28"/70cm	1
E	Row 2 working cord	44"/110cm	2
F	Row 2 (outer petals) filler cord	44"/110cm	1
G	Row 3 working cord	59"/150cm	3

1 The sample in the photo is made of soft jute cord and measures 3¼"/8cm in diameter. The length of cord required will vary with its weight, but the table above can be a guide.

2

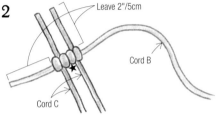

Leaving a short tail at the beginning end of each cord, tie a Horizontal Clove Hitch over filler cord B with each cord C.

3

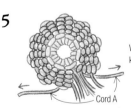

Fold back the filler cord and tie a Horizontal Clove Hitch over it with each cord C.

4

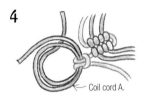

Coil cord A into a double circle. Attach the long end of cord B to it using a Lark's Head Knot. This completes 1 petal.

5

In this manner, add 8 more petals to the cord A circle. Then, with cord B, make 1 more Lark's Head Knot through the circle. Pull the ends of cord A to tighten the center.

6

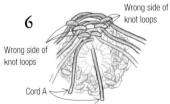

Turn the piece over. Weave the ends of cords C through the loops of the Clove Hitches. Weave the ends of cords A and B through the loops of the Lark's Head Knots.

7 Follow the Knotting Diagram to add the middle band of petals: Use cord D as the filler and cord E to tie the Clove Hitch knots. After shaping 2 petals, use a Lark's Head Knot to attach cord D to cord B, between 2 petals of the inner band. Complete the middle band in this way and weave the cord ends into the wrong side.

8 Now add the outer band of petals: Use cord F as the filler cord and cord G to tie the Clove Hitch knots. After shaping 3 petals, use a Lark's Head Knot to attach cord F to cord D, between 2 petals of the middle band. Complete the outer band in this way and weave in the cord ends on the wrong side.

---

(68) Square Knot Braided Band

Two identical bands (A and B), each made with 2 sennits joined at intervals, are interlocked. Look at the photo to see how the bands overlap consistently.

photo page 93

❧ Knotting Diagram

A and B are knotted separately but interwoven.

Knotting Technique

Left-facing Square Knot → page 31

(69) Vertical Clove Hitch Tapestry

(70) Cavandoli Snowflake Tapestry

(69) A Native American-style geometric pattern made with 3 colors, all tied in Vertical Clove Hitches.

(70) Both Vertical and Horizontal Clove Hitches are used for this tapestry—one for each color.

69 Vertical Clove Hitch Tapestry

This 3-color design with a Native American motif is worked entirely in Vertical Clove Hitches. The filler (vertical) cords extend into a fringe; make them whatever color you like.

photo page 96

❀ Knotting Diagram

Color A (also vertical cords) → ☐ Attach horizontal cord. ☐ → / ←☐ Cut horizontal cord.

Color A →
Color B →
Color C →

Weave in unused cord on the back

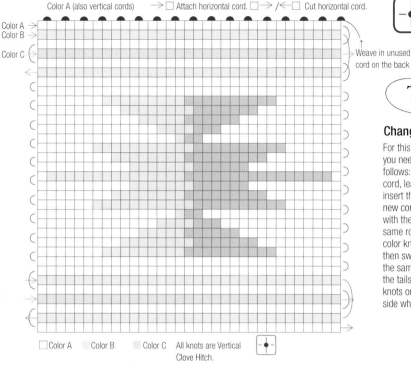

☐ Color A ▨ Color B ▨ Color C   All knots are Vertical Clove Hitch.   ⊡

Knotting Technique

⊡ Vertical Clove Hitch → page 66

Tip-1

Change colors smoothly

For this and similar Vertical Clove Hitch designs where you need to change cord color within a row, work as follows: Tie the first loop of the knot with the new color cord, leaving a short tail on the back of the work. Then insert the old color in between the filler cord and the new cord and complete the second loop of the knot with the new color. If you need the old color again in the same row, repeat this action to carry it inside the new-color knots to the spot where it will next be used, and then switch colors in the same way. Tuck the tails inside the knots on the wrong side when finished.

New color

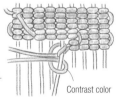

Tip-2

Neatly carry colors from row to row

If the spot where the color changes aligns from row to row (as for a vertical stripe), simply rest the cord until it's needed in the next row and then incorporate it as described above right in Tip 01. If the colors do not align vertically, here is what to do:

For fewer contrast-color knots on the next row

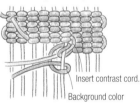

Insert contrast cord.
Background color

Contrast color

① Tie the knots up to the point where the contrast color ended in the row above. Bring the contrast color cord down and insert it in the next knot as shown (same as in Tip 01). If the contrast color is not need for the next knot, carry it inside subsequent knots until it is needed.

② When you are ready to use the contrast color, tie the first loop of the knot, insert the background color cord, and complete the knot.

For more contrast-color knots on the next row

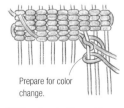

Prepare for color change.

Contrast color

① Plan ahead while working the row above the one where you need to add contrast color knots: Carry the contrast color cord inside the background color knots until it is above the place where you will need it.

② On the next row, when you are ready to change colors, bring the contrast color down, tie the first loop of the knot, insert the background color cord, and complete the knot.

Tip-3

Change color and knot direction too

You can also use a Horizontal Clove Hitch to work a contrasting color, as in the Snowflake Tapestry on the opposite page. Here's how to attach it; there are more details on p. 98.

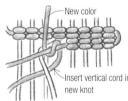

New color

Insert vertical cord in new knot

① Tie the first loop of the knot with the new color cord. Then insert the vertical cord between the filler cord and the new cord and complete the second loop of the knot with the new color.

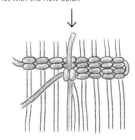

② Follow your chart to make the required number of Horizontal Clove Hitches in the new color, carrying the old color cord inside the knots until it is needed again.

70 Cavandoli Snowflake Tapestry

Tapestries made with both Horizontal and Vertical Clove Hitches are known as Cavandoli work. The cord used to tie the Vertical knots is also the filler cord for the Horizontal knots.

photo page 96

Knotting Diagram

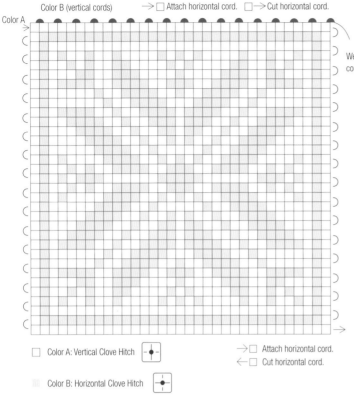

Color A
Color B (vertical cords)
→ ☐ Attach horizontal cord.   ☐→ Cut horizontal cord.

Weave in unused cord on the back.

☐ Color A: Vertical Clove Hitch
☐ Color B: Horizontal Clove Hitch

→☐ Attach horizontal cord.
←☐ Cut horizontal cord.

Knotting Technique

Vertical Clove Hitch → page 66   Horizontal Clove Hitch → page 66

Tip   Cavandoli: Practice first

At first glance it may be confusing to see how a cord changes from working cord to filler cord and back again in order to create the colorful geometric patterns of Cavandoli work. Once you work this little sample you'll have the hang of the technique. The step photos below demonstrate the process (cord lengths in inches).

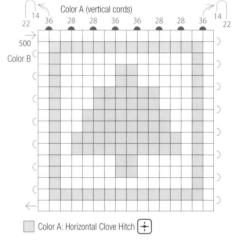

Color A (vertical cords)
14 22 36 28 28 36 36 28 28 36 14 22
500
Color B

☐ Color A: Horizontal Clove Hitch
☐ Color B: Vertical Clove Hitch

Try your hand at the pine tree sample

As you work, remember the white background is made entirely of Vertical Clove Hitches and the contrast pattern is made of Horizontal Clove Hitches tied over the white cord.

Attach 16 vertical cords in Color A (green) to an anchor cord. Make a row of Vertical Clove Hitches with Color B.

To begin row 2, make a Vertical Clove Hitch with Color B, then lay Color B across the work.

To complete row 2, use Color A to make 14 Horizontal Clove Hitches over Color B; then use Color B to make 1 Vertical Clove Hitch.

Continue, following the chart and switching from Vertical to Horizontal knots as indicated by the color changes.

The knotting is complete and the design is clear.

Turn the work over and use a tapestry needle to weave the tails of the cords into the knots. You can leave the fringe if you like.

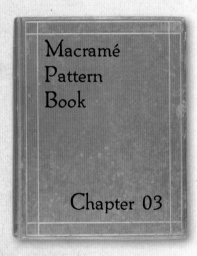

Macramé
Pattern
Book

Chapter 03

Projects

How to Read the Project Directions

In Chapter 03 you'll find an array of small items to make,
each incorporates one or more of the knots or knotted
patterns in Chapter 02. Here's how to follow the codes for
making them:

01. (22) → button

• The first number is the item I.D.; later in this chapter it
precedes the directions for the item.

• The circled number (or sometimes numbers) is the knot
or motif I.D. as given in Chapter 02 (there's also an index
to the knot directions on p. 6). Look back at Chapter 02 for
how to make these.

• The word at the end is the item's name.

cute and easy

Little knotted items make great fashion embellishments. These are so simple and so sweet, make lots to use with different outfits or to give to friends.

D

E

B

C

A

01. (22) → button

01. [button]   Make brightly colored Awaji Knot buttons to spice up a jacket or sweater. how to make ... page 125

02. [flower brooch]   Add a pin back to this cute Lark's Head flower for a delicate lapel or scarf pin. how to make ... page 125

02. ⑨ → flower brooch

B

03. ㉛ → leaf brooch

A

04. ⑨ ㉛ → corsage

B

03. [leaf brooch]　We recommend this small leaf brooch as an accent for a hat or bag.　how to make … page 126

04. [corsage]　If you combine the flower and leaf, you can make an adorable corsage.　how to make … page 126

fashion accents from favorite knots

Once you've found your favorite patterns and knots, we recommend you start by making something small with several cords. It is especially enjoyable to make something you can wear or use every day.

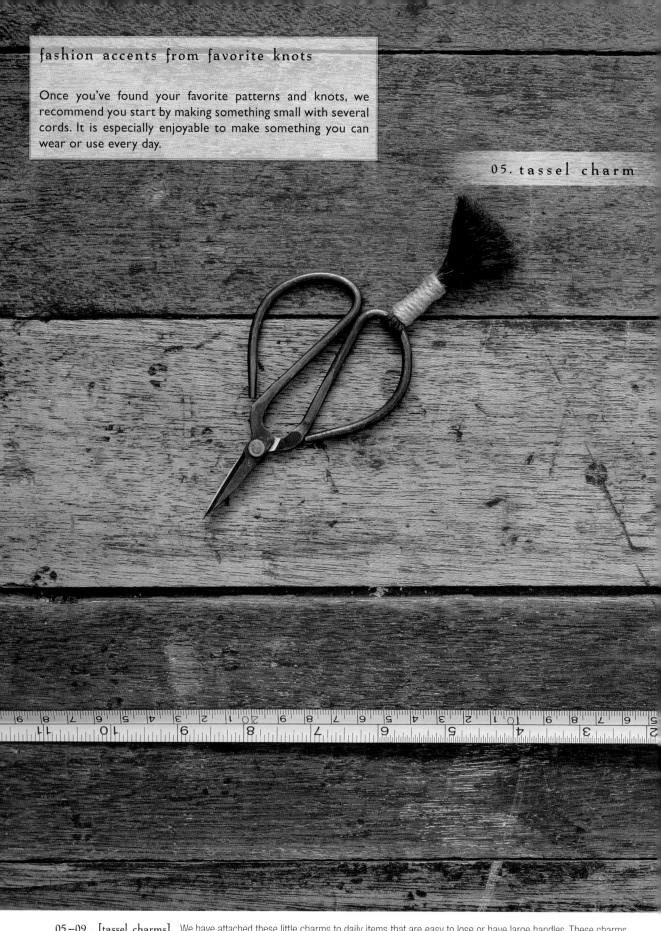

05-09 . [tassel charms]   We have attached these little charms to daily items that are easy to lose or have large handles. These charms don't require much cord, so they're a good use of leftover bits. Make them uniquely yours by using your favorite colors.   how to make ... page 132-133

07. ⑫ → tassel charm

08. ㉑ → tassel charm

09. ⑥ → tassel charm

06. ⑰ → tassel charm

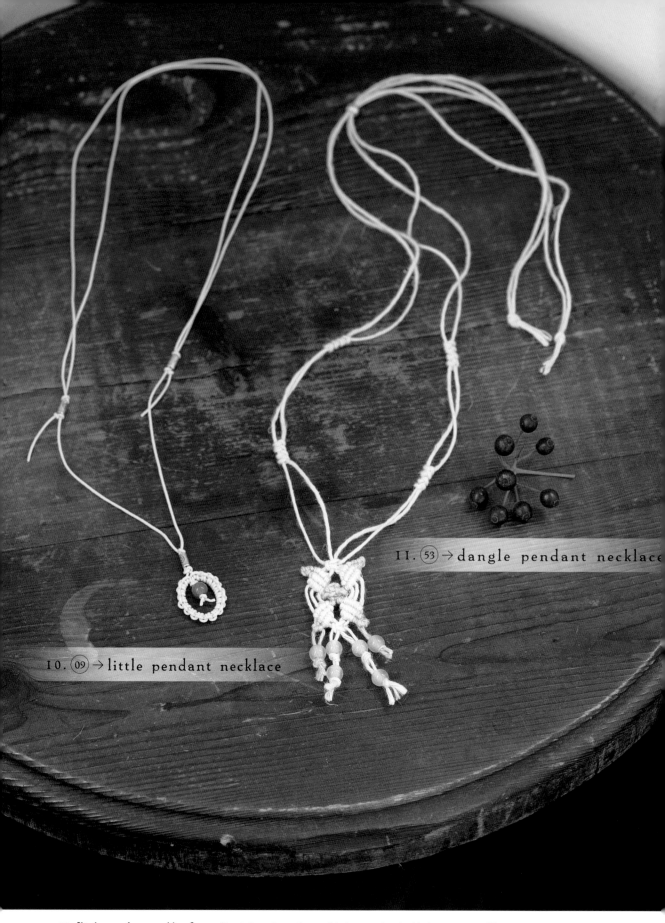

II. ⑤③ → dangle pendant necklace

10. ⑨ → little pendant necklace

10. [little pendant necklace]   Simple to make and wear, this is a great project to try your new skills on.
how to make ... page 127

II. [dangle pendant necklace]   We used the Leaf-and-Bud Mesh pattern as a pendant for a necklace
(now it looks like a flower). how to make ... page 128

12. (44) → lacy choker

13. (12) → spiral choker

12. [lacy choker]   A fine cord makes a delicate choker knotted in a diamond pattern and embellished with beads and a flower charm.
how to make ... page 129

13. [spiral choker]   A charming choker made with Double Left-twist Spiral Knots in red and white, with a pretty silver charm.
how to make ... page 130

14. 61 63 → lacy belt

15. 04 → braided belt

14. [lacy belt]   Alternate 2 woven diamond patterns to make a stunning belt. Try a thicker cord if you'd like it chunkier.
                    how to make ... page 131

15. [braided belt] Flat leather "lace" cords make a handsome 6-ply Braid. Go for suede instead of smooth leather if you prefer.
                    how to make ... page 131

17. (01) (37) → f l o w e r d o t b r a c e l e t

16. (19) (47) → c h e v r o n b r a c e l e t

16. [chevron bracelet]   These colorful friendship bracelets have a Native American look.   how to make ... page 134

17. [flower dot bracelet]   These are also friendship bracelets, but their tiny floral pattern gives them the flavor of a sweet Alpine ribbon.   how to make ... page 135

easy add-ons made from macramé

Add macramé straps to jazz up items such as bags, watches, or cameras. Choose your favorite colors and cords-in a good weight of course. Be creative, our ideas are just the beginning!

18. ⑳ → braided handle

19. ⑤ ㉒ → medallion handle

18. [braided handle]   It's easy to customize the handles on bags with grommets. This simple round braid lends a grown-up finish. how to make ... page 136

19. [medallion handle]   The Awaji Knot adds distinction to a plain Square Knot handle; fringe adds extra flair.
how to make ... page 136

20. (48) → zigzag strap

20. [zigzag strap] This long strap can be worn crossed diagonally over the body, or doubled up to make a shoulder bag.
how to make ... page 137

21. [watchbands] Who could resist these distinctive knotted watchbands? Each has great texture and character.
how to make ... page 138

22. (05) (45) → c a m e r a s t r a p

22. [camera strap] Knotted in forest-colored hemp cord, this strap is both soft and strong enough to hold the camera.
how to make ... page 139

23. [lacy edging]   Dress up a plain stole, scarf, or even a cami with this knotted edging that resembles vintage tatting.
how to make ... page 140

24. (41) (60) (64) → fringed diamond border

24. [fringed diamond border]   Inspired by the Eastern European fabric on p. 9, we added a red fringe to a tablecloth.
how to make ... page 141

There are so many possible directions in which to take macramé, your head can spin with the options. Explore variations in color, texture, or scale. Combine several patterns. Make something utilitarian or something fanciful. Following are projects that will build your skills, please your eye, and be nice to use too.

A

26. ㉝→striped hot pad

B

25. ㉸→nordic coaster

25. [nordic coaster]   Our simple snowflake tapestry is good to go as coaster. Make a pair with positive/negative coloring.
how to make ... page 142

26. [striped hot pad]   The Twisted Buddhist Treasure Mesh is easy to make in stripes and nice and chunky: perfect for a small mat.
how to make ... page 143

27. ⓺⑥ → r o u n d   m a t

27. [round mat]   Make the round flower motif as large and colorful as you like (whatever suits your decor) and place atop a chair or stool.
how to make ... page 144

28. ⑤ ㉕ → n e t b a g

28. [net bag] A bright color and easy knots make such quick, fun work of this loose net bag you'll want to craft a slew of them.
how to make ... page 146

29. (05) (24) → m i n i   t o t e

29. [mini tote] At 8"/20cm square, this petite bag makes a perfectly ladylike carrier for your phone and a few other essentials.
how to make ... page 148

30. (23) (46) → diamond tote bag

30. [diamond tote bag] Discreetly graphic red accents peak through a diamond mesh pattern on this smart midsize tote.
how to make ... page 150

31. ㉓ ㉖ → s m a l l   s t r i p e d   b a g

31. [small striped bag] This neatly striped little bag is the perfect size for your lunch—or a bottle of wine, a corkscrew, and 2 cups.
how to make ... page 152

32. (05)(23)(35)(54)→ h a r v e s t   b a s k e t

32. [harvest basket]   An oval basket made from a rustic cord such as raffia. Use in your home to hold napkins or macramé cords or outside to hold lunch or snacks for a picnic.   how to make ... page 154

33. (58) → retro handbag

33. [retro handbag] A terrific nubby pattern lends chic personality to this classic bag. It's intriguing and not as challenging to make as you might suppose. how to make ... page 156

project instructions

01. button   photo ... page 100

photo ... page 100

pattern: (22)

materials

For each button, 1 piece round leather cord (2mm), 32"/80cm long
(shown in A: Caramel; B: Blue, C: Dark Red; D: Sand; E: Yellow Green)
1 shank button for each

size

1" x 1"/2.5 x 2.5cm

tip

Shape the Awaji Knot into a dome so that it will cup the shank button: Tap the wrong side of the knot with your finger and then pull the cord tight, rounding the knot slightly.

[instructions]

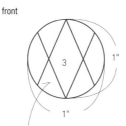

front

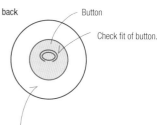

back

Button

Check fit of button.

① Make the Awaji Knot with 3 passes of the cords (as shown at the bottom of p. 47). Tap your finger on the back to make a dome shape.

② Bring the cord ends to the back, cut flush with surface, and seal with glue.

③ Attach the button

Apply glue to face of button and press it into the cupped knot.

Paper clip

Secure with a large paper clip until the glue dries.

Starting method

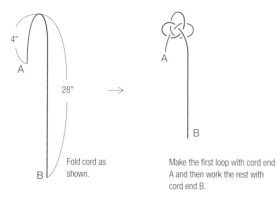

4"

A

28"

→

A

B

B

Fold cord as shown.

Make the first loop with cord end A and then work the rest with cord end B.

---

02. flower brooch   photo ... page 100

photo ... page 100

pattern: (09)

materials

For each flower, 1 piece extra-fine cotton cord (0.5–0.7mm), 52"/130cm long
(shown in A: Off White; B: Orange)
1 round 6mm bead (semi-precious stone)
(shown in A: Peach Aventurine; B: Rose Quartz)
1 brooch pin for each

size

1" x 1"/2.5 x 2.5cm

tip

The ends of the petals are accented with Picots. If you'd like a lacier edge, you can add Picots between other knots too – experiment.

[instructions]

① Fold the cord as shown.

12"

Filler cord

Working cord

☆

40"

② Make 1 Vertical Lark's Head Knot (→p. 35).

☆

③ Knot the inner section.

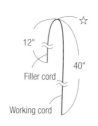

☆

❷ Pass the filler cord through the loop marked ☆.

¼"

❶ Make 4 Vertical Lark's Head Knots, with Picots in between.

④ Knot the first petal.

3 knots

¼"

3 knots

Pass filler cord through picot.

⑤ Knot the remaining petals.

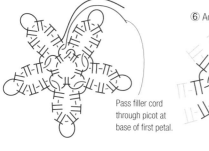

Pass filler cord through picot at base of first petal.

⑥ Add a bead to the center.

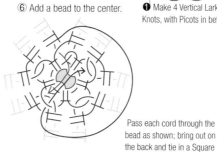

Pass each cord through the bead as shown; bring out on the back and tie in a Square Knot (→p. 21); cut excess.

⑦ Attach the brooch pin to the back.

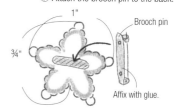

1"

Brooch pin

¾"

Affix with glue.

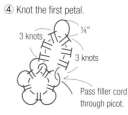

03. leaf brooch   photo ... page 101

photo ... page 101

pattern: 51

materials
(Straight Leaf)
Moss green extra-fine cotton cord (0.5–0.7mm)
   1 piece 24"/60cm long
   5 pieces 12"/30cm long

(3-Lobe Leaf)
Moss Green or Brown Multi extra-fine cotton cord (0.5–0.7mm)
   3 pieces 20"/50cm long
   1 piece 18"/45cm long
   1 piece 12"/30cm long
1 brooch pin for each

size
(Straight Leaf) 1¼" x ⅝" /3 x 1.5cm
(3-Lobe Leaf) 1½" x 1½"/3.7 x 3.7cm

tip
The wrapped binding that secures each stem gives a sweet finish to these make-believe leaves.

① Start at the tip, in detail

At the center of the cord, make an Overhand Knot and pull tight.

Added cord

Add another cord, centering it below the knot. Tie the second cord to the first with Vertical Clove Hitches (→p. 66).

③ Wrap the stem, in detail

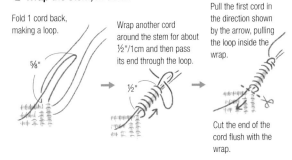

Fold 1 cord back, making a loop.

⅝"

Wrap another cord around the stem for about ½"/1cm and then pass its end through the loop.

½"

Pull the first cord in the direction shown by the arrow, pulling the loop inside the wrap.

Cut the end of the cord flush with the wrap.

[instructions]

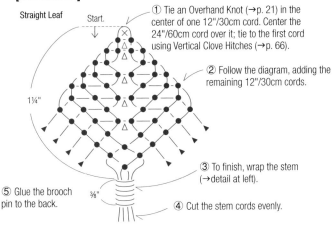

Straight Leaf

Start.

1¼"

⅜"

① Tie an Overhand Knot (→p. 21) in the center of one 12"/30cm cord. Center the 24"/60cm cord over it; tie to the first cord using Vertical Clove Hitches (→p. 66).

② Follow the diagram, adding the remaining 12"/30cm cords.

③ To finish, wrap the stem (→detail at left).

⑤ Glue the brooch pin to the back.

④ Cut the stem cords evenly.

▷ Add 12"/30cm cord here.
▷ Add 24"/60cm cord here.

▶ Weave cord ends into knots on back (→p. 23).

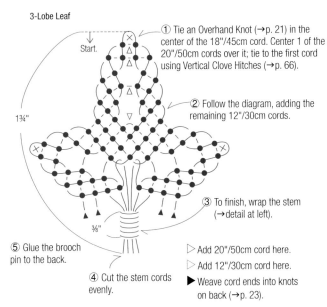

3-Lobe Leaf

Start.

1¾"

⅜"

① Tie an Overhand Knot (→p. 21) in the center of the 18"/45cm cord. Center 1 of the 20"/50cm cords over it; tie to the first cord using Vertical Clove Hitches (→p. 66).

② Follow the diagram, adding the remaining 12"/30cm cords.

③ To finish, wrap the stem (→detail at left).

⑤ Glue the brooch pin to the back.

④ Cut the stem cords evenly.

▷ Add 20"/50cm cord here.
▷ Add 12"/30cm cord here.
▶ Weave cord ends into knots on back (→p. 23).

---

04. corsage   photo ... page 101

photo ... page 101

pattern: 09 51

materials
02: One Flower (→p. 125), complete through step 6.
03: Two Straight Leaves (above), complete through step 2.
1 brooch pin

size
1⅝" x 1⅝"/4 x 4cm

tip
When you make the Flower, don't trim the excess cord length. For the Leaves, finish the edges but leave all the stem cords. You'll need these to assemble the Corsage.

[instructions]

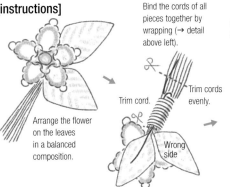

Arrange the flower on the leaves in a balanced composition.

Bind the cords of all pieces together by wrapping (→ detail above left).

Trim cord.

Trim cords evenly.

Wrong side

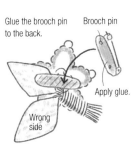

Glue the brooch pin to the back.

Brooch pin

Apply glue.

Wrong side

10. little pendant necklace   photo ... page 104

photo ... page 104

materials

Off-white extra-fine cotton cord (0.5–0.7mm):

    1 piece 12"/30cm long (filler cord)

    1 piece 59"/150cm long

1 round 6mm bead (shown in Aventurine, semi-precious stone)

3 engraved silver tubular 5mm x 3mm beads

size

Adjustable

tip

The Gathering Knot used to secure the cords at each side creates an adjustable closure that requires no clasp or other finding (→below left).

[instructions]

⑤ Gathering Knot, in detail

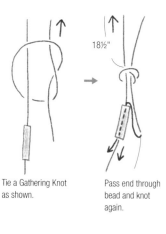

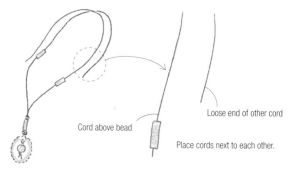

Cord above bead

Loose end of other cord

Place cords next to each other.

18½"

Tie a Gathering Knot as shown.

Pass end through bead and knot again.

Repeat on the other side with the other loose cord end.

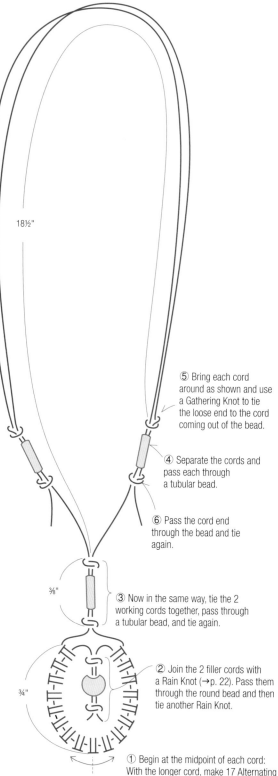

18½"

⑤ Bring each cord around as shown and use a Gathering Knot to tie the loose end to the cord coming out of the bead.

④ Separate the cords and pass each through a tubular bead.

⑥ Pass the cord end through the bead and tie again.

⅜"

③ Now in the same way, tie the 2 working cords together, pass through a tubular bead, and tie again.

¾"

② Join the 2 filler cords with a Rain Knot (→p. 22). Pass them through the round bead and then tie another Rain Knot.

Start.

① Begin at the midpoint of each cord: With the longer cord, make 17 Alternating Vertical Lark's Head Knots (→p. 35) over the shorter cord.

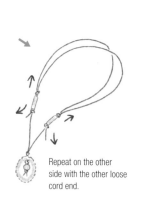

materials

Natural-color fine hemp twine (1.2mm):
    2 pieces 16"/40cm long (filler cords)
    4 pieces 40"/100cm long
Rose fine hemp twine: 2 pieces 32"/80cm long
6 round 6mm bead (shown in Rose Quartz, semi-precious stone)
1 engraved silver round 6mm bead

size

Adjustable

tip

The starting point is at the tip of the upper leaves on both sides: Leave
1¼"/3cm at the end of each filler cord; tie each in a temporary knot and
pin to your board about 1"/2.5cm apart so you can set up the design
proportions.

[instructions]

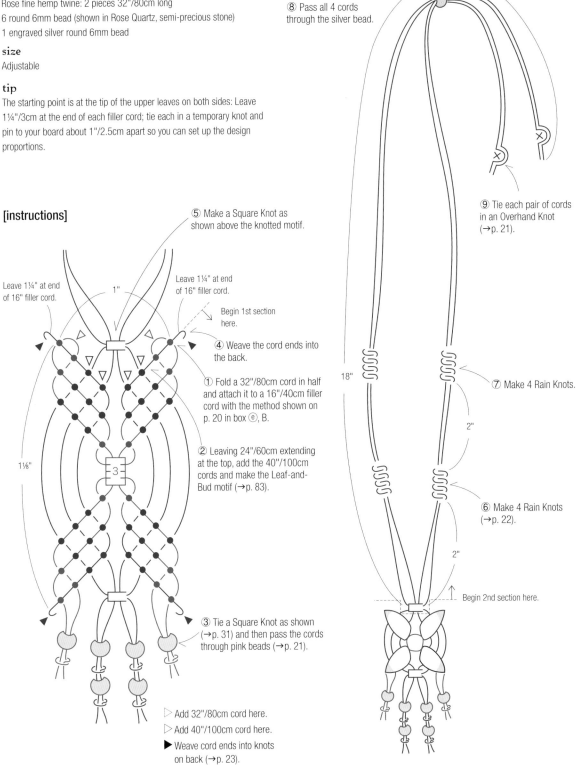

⑤ Make a Square Knot as shown above the knotted motif.

Leave 1¼" at end of 16" filler cord.   1"   Leave 1¼" at end of 16" filler cord.

Begin 1st section here.

④ Weave the cord ends into the back.

① Fold a 32"/80cm cord in half and attach it to a 16"/40cm filler cord with the method shown on p. 20 in box ⓔ, B.

② Leaving 24"/60cm extending at the top, add the 40"/100cm cords and make the Leaf-and-Bud motif (→p. 83).

1⅛"

3

③ Tie a Square Knot as shown (→p. 31) and then pass the cords through pink beads (→p. 21).

▷ Add 32"/80cm cord here.
▷ Add 40"/100cm cord here.
▶ Weave cord ends into knots on back (→p. 23).

⑧ Pass all 4 cords through the silver bead.

⑨ Tie each pair of cords in an Overhand Knot (→p. 21).

18"

⑦ Make 4 Rain Knots.

2"

⑥ Make 4 Rain Knots (→p. 22).

2"

Begin 2nd section here.

12. lacy choker   photo ... page 105

materials
Beige extra-fine cotton cord (0.5–0.7mm): 4 pieces 120"/300cm long
4 engraved silver 4mm x 6mm beads
1 engraved silver 15mm diameter flower
1 engraved silver 9mm x 10mm bell

size
⅝" x 15¾"/1.5cm x 40cm

tip
The diagram shows 31 repeats of the diamond pattern. Test fit the choker as you knot. Adjust the length as you wish.

[instructions]

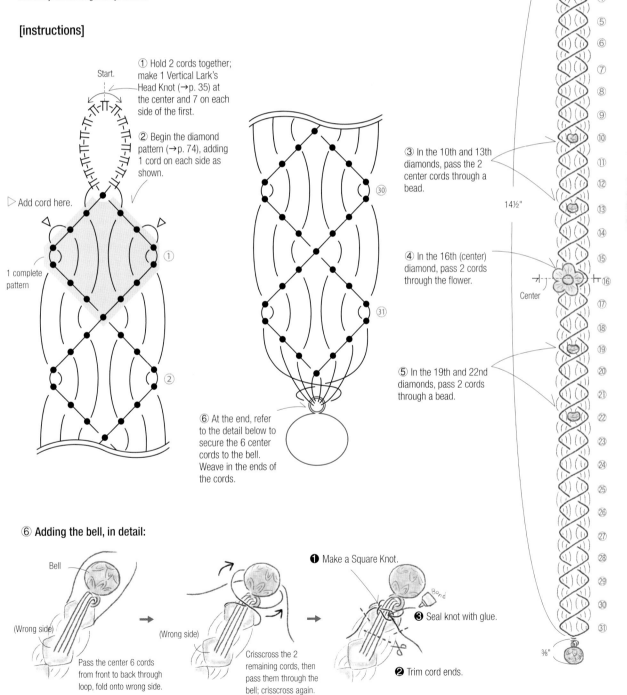

① Hold 2 cords together; make 1 Vertical Lark's Head Knot (→p. 35) at the center and 7 on each side of the first.

② Begin the diamond pattern (→p. 74), adding 1 cord on each side as shown.

Start.

▷ Add cord here.

1 complete pattern

③ In the 10th and 13th diamonds, pass the 2 center cords through a bead.

④ In the 16th (center) diamond, pass 2 cords through the flower.

⑤ In the 19th and 22nd diamonds, pass 2 cords through a bead.

⑥ At the end, refer to the detail below to secure the 6 center cords to the bell. Weave in the ends of the cords.

Center

14½"

¾"

⅜"

① ② ③ ④ ⑤ ⑥ ⑦ ⑧ ⑨ ⑩ ⑪ ⑫ ⑬ ⑭ ⑮ ⑯ ⑰ ⑱ ⑲ ⑳ ㉑ ㉒ ㉓ ㉔ ㉕ ㉖ ㉗ ㉘ ㉙ ㉚ ㉛

Chapter 03   Projects

⑥ Adding the bell, in detail:

Bell

(Wrong side)

Pass the center 6 cords from front to back through loop, fold onto wrong side.

(Wrong side)

Crisscross the 2 remaining cords, then pass them through the bell; crisscross again.

❶ Make a Square Knot.

❸ Seal knot with glue.

❷ Trim cord ends.

Bond

13. spiral choker   photo ... page 105

materials

Natural-color medium-weight hemp twine (1.8mm):
- 2 pieces 20"/50cm long (filler cords)
- 2 pieces 71"/180cm long (working cords A)

Red medium-weight hemp twine (1.8mm)
- 2 pieces 71"/180cm long (working cords B)

1 engraved silver 9mm x 10mm bell
4 engraved silver 4mm x 6mm beads
1 engraved silver 4mm terminator clasp

size

15¾"/40cm long

tip

To start by placing the bell in the middle of the choker, read p. 19, box ⓓ. To wrap the cords before adding the clasp, read "Wrapping the stem, in detail" (→p. 126).

⑥ **Attaching the clasp, in detail**

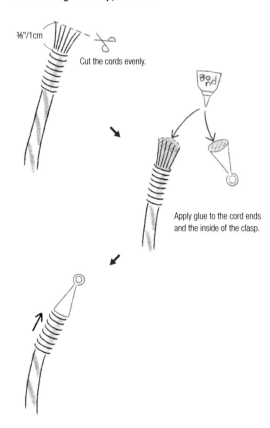

⅜"/1cm

Cut the cords evenly.

Apply glue to the cord ends and the inside of the clasp.

[instructions]

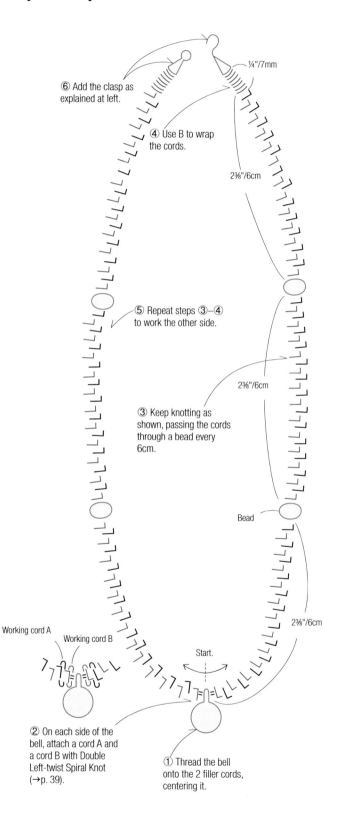

⑥ Add the clasp as explained at left.

¼"/7mm

④ Use B to wrap the cords.

2⅜"/6cm

⑤ Repeat steps ③–④ to work the other side.

2⅜"/6cm

③ Keep knotting as shown, passing the cords through a bead every 6cm.

Bead

2⅜"/6cm

Working cord A

Working cord B

Start.

② On each side of the bell, attach a cord A and a cord B with Double Left-twist Spiral Knot (→p. 39).

① Thread the bell onto the 2 filler cords, centering it.

14. lacy belt   pattern:

photo ... page 106

materials

Dark Green round leather cord (2mm):
   3 pieces 9 yards/800cm long; 1 piece 6 yards/540cm long;
   2 pieces 12"/30cm long
One 1"/2.5cm wood ring

size

1¼" x 32"/3cm x 82cm (not including the 20"/50cm fringe)

tip

Two woven diamond patterns alternate to make this belt. Note that while each is worked on fewer cords than shown for its directions on p. 90 or p. 91, the basic process is the same. You can cut the fringe at the length you like.

15. braided belt   pattern: 04

photo ... page 106

materials

Brown flat leather cord (3mm): 3 pieces 4 yards/360cm long
One 1"/2.5cm cast pewter ring

size

⅝" x 35"/1.5cm x 89cm (not including the 20"/50cm fringe)

tip

The fringe on this belt is just extra length from the cords in the braided section. Easy! Simply make a small wrapped binding to secure the braid and leave the extending cords long for the fringe.

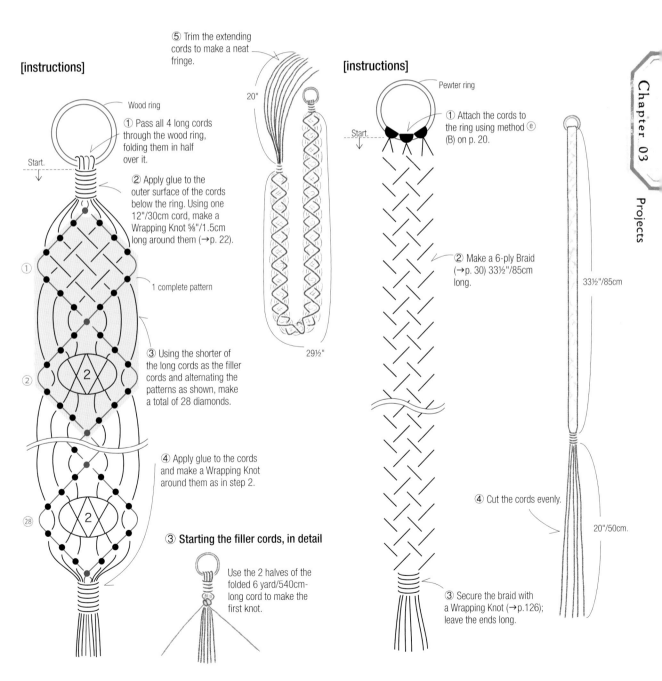

[instructions]

Wood ring

① Pass all 4 long cords through the wood ring, folding them in half over it.

Start.

② Apply glue to the outer surface of the cords below the ring. Using one 12"/30cm cord, make a Wrapping Knot ⅝"/1.5cm long around them (→p. 22).

1 complete pattern

③ Using the shorter of the long cords as the filler cords and alternating the patterns as shown, make a total of 28 diamonds.

④ Apply glue to the cords and make a Wrapping Knot around them as in step 2.

⑤ Trim the extending cords to make a neat fringe.

20"

29½"

③ Starting the filler cords, in detail

Use the 2 halves of the folded 6 yard/540cm-long cord to make the first knot.

[instructions]

Pewter ring

① Attach the cords to the ring using method ⓔ (B) on p. 20.

Start.

② Make a 6-ply Braid (→p. 30) 33½"/85cm long.

33½"/85cm

④ Cut the cords evenly.

20"/50cm.

③ Secure the braid with a Wrapping Knot (→p.126); leave the ends long.

05. tassel charm   photo ... page 102

Wrapping Knot → page 22

materials
Soft jute cord (2mm):
    5 pieces Brown 6"/15cm long
    1 piece Yellow Ochre 16"/40cm long

size
2"/5cm long

tip
This tassel is made by simply doubling cords over a ring and it is very easy to adjust the size: Use as many cords as give you the bulk you like and cut them a little more than twice the length you want.

[instructions]

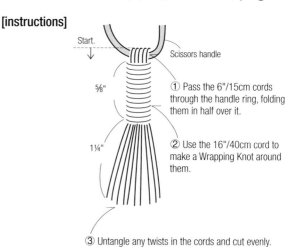

Start.
Scissors handle
⅝"
1¼"

① Pass the 6"/15cm cords through the handle ring, folding them in half over it.

② Use the 16"/40cm cord to make a Wrapping Knot around them.

③ Untangle any twists in the cords and cut evenly.

---

07. tassel charm   photo ... page 103

pattern: 12

materials
White soft jute cord (2mm):
    1 piece 20"/50cm long; 2 pieces 8"/20cm long (for filler cords)
Red soft jute cord (2mm):
    1 piece 20"/50cm long; 1 piece 8"/20cm long (for filler cord)
1 silver-color 12mm split ring

size
3¼"/8cm long

tip
This tassel gets a polished look from the braided filler cords that support the Double Left-twist Spiral Knots (→p. 39).

[instructions]

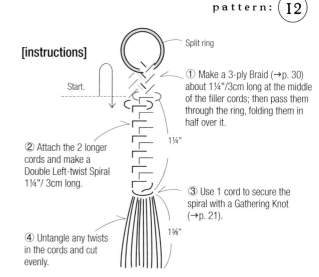

Split ring
Start.
1¼"
1⅜"

① Make a 3-ply Braid (→p. 30) about 1¼"/3cm long at the middle of the filler cords; then pass them through the ring, folding them in half over it.

② Attach the 2 longer cords and make a Double Left-twist Spiral 1¼"/ 3cm long.

③ Use 1 cord to secure the spiral with a Gathering Knot (→p. 21).

④ Untangle any twists in the cords and cut evenly.

---

09. tassel charm   photo ... page 103

pattern: 06

materials
Soft jute cord (2mm):
    1 piece each Red and Indigo, 24"/60cm long
    1 piece White, 16"/40cm long
1 silver-color 12mm split ring

size
3½"/9cm long

tip
The key to creating the alternating color pattern is to line the cords up carefully after placing over the ring, before you start the Square Knots, as shown in the step 3 detail.

[instructions]

③ Cord sequence, in detail

Indigo   Indigo

Red White   Red White

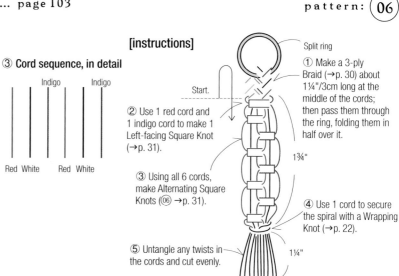

Split ring
Start.
1¾"
1¼"

① Make a 3-ply Braid (→p. 30) about 1¼"/3cm long at the middle of the cords; then pass them through the ring, folding them in half over it.

② Use 1 red cord and 1 indigo cord to make 1 Left-facing Square Knot (→p. 31).

③ Using all 6 cords, make Alternating Square Knots (06 →p. 31).

④ Use 1 cord to secure the spiral with a Wrapping Knot (→p. 22).

⑤ Untangle any twists in the cords and cut evenly.

06. tassel charm   photo ... page 103

photo ... page 103

pattern: **17**

materials
Olive Green soft jute cord (2mm):
 1 piece 20"/50cm long; 1 piece 8"/20cm long (filler cord)
Soft 3-ply Forest Green jute cord: 1 piece 20"/50cm long

size
3⅛"/8cm long

tip
Here a Round 4-ply Lanyard Knot is worked around 2 filler cords, making the resulting braid a bit fatter than usual. Refer to the step 3 detail, below, to see how it's done.

③ **Braiding around a filler, in detail**

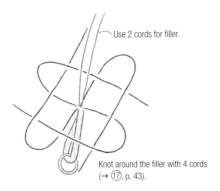

Use 2 cords for filler.

Knot around the filler with 4 cords
(→ ⑰, p. 43).

[instructions]

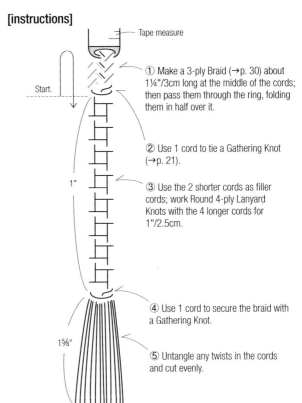

Tape measure

Start.

① Make a 3-ply Braid (→p. 30) about 1¼"/3cm long at the middle of the cords; then pass them through the ring, folding them in half over it.

② Use 1 cord to tie a Gathering Knot (→p. 21).

③ Use the 2 shorter cords as filler cords; work Round 4-ply Lanyard Knots with the 4 longer cords for 1"/2.5cm.

1"

④ Use 1 cord to secure the braid with a Gathering Knot.

1⅝"

⑤ Untangle any twists in the cords and cut evenly.

08. tassel charm   photo ... page 103

photo ... page 103

pattern: **21**

materials
Soft jute cord (2mm):
 1 piece each White, Brick, Orange, and Brown, 20"/50cm long
1 silver-color 12mm split ring

size
3½"/9cm long

tip
A 4-ply Braid folds through the split loop, below it the cords are worked in a Square Herringbone Braid (→ ㉑, p. 47), where there is a tip for sequencing the colors.

[instructions]

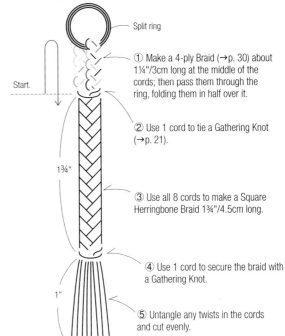

Split ring

Start.

① Make a 4-ply Braid (→p. 30) about 1¼"/3cm long at the middle of the cords; then pass them through the ring, folding them in half over it.

② Use 1 cord to tie a Gathering Knot (→p. 21).

1¾"

③ Use all 8 cords to make a Square Herringbone Braid 1¾"/4.5cm long.

④ Use 1 cord to secure the braid with a Gathering Knot.

1"

⑤ Untangle any twists in the cords and cut evenly.

materials

Middle sample:

Green fine hemp twine (1.2mm): 2 pieces 47"/120cm long (a)

Moss Green fine hemp twine (1.2mm):
2 pieces 47"/120cm long (b)

Red fine hemp twine (1.2mm): 2 pieces 47"/120cm long (c)

Natural-color fine hemp twine (1.2mm):
2 pieces 47"/120cm long (d)

1 engraved silver 4mm x 6mm bead

Top sample:

Indigo fine hemp twine (1.2mm): 2 pieces 47"/120cm long (a)

Rose fine hemp twine (1.2mm): 2 pieces 47"/120cm long (b)

Natural-color fine hemp twine (1.2mm):
4 pieces 47"/120cm long (c, d)

1 engraved silver 4mm x 6mm bead

Bottom sample:

Moss Green fine hemp twine (1.2mm):
2 pieces 47"/120cm long (a)

Yellow fine hemp twine (1.2mm): 2 pieces 47"/120cm long (b)

Dark Brown fine hemp twine (1.2mm):
2 pieces 47"/120cm long (c)

Natural-color fine hemp twine (1.2mm):
2 pieces 47"/120cm long (d)

1 engraved silver 4mm x 6mm bead

size

⅝" x 12½"/1.5cm x 32cm

tip

Begin at the middle of the bracelet, threading the bead onto the 4 middle cords, and work out toward both ends. Keep watching carefully to make sure the pattern is made up of nice, neat nested V shapes.

① Starting off, in detail

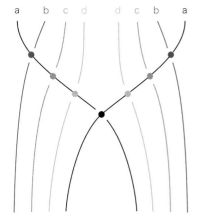

Each V-shape counts as 1 row.

[instructions]

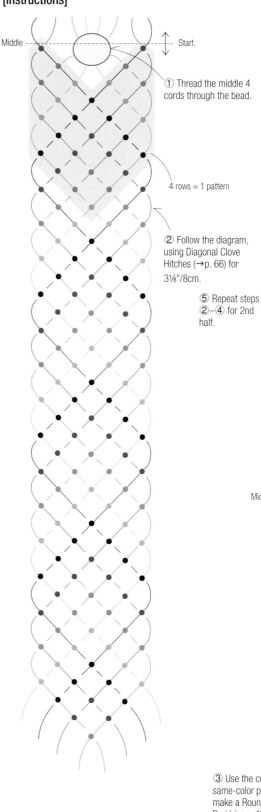

Middle ---- Start.

① Thread the middle 4 cords through the bead.

4 rows = 1 pattern

② Follow the diagram, using Diagonal Clove Hitches (→p. 66) for 3⅛"/8cm.

⑤ Repeat steps ②–④ for 2nd half.

Middle ----

3⅛"

③ Use the cords in same-color pairs to make a Round 4-ply Braid (→p. 46) for 2¾"/7cm.

2¾"

④ Use 1 cord to secure the braid with a Wrapping Knot (→p. 22).

⅜"

I7. flower dot bracelet photo ... page I07

materials

Top sample:
  Red fine hemp twine (1.2mm):
    2 pieces 40"/100cm long (a)
  Red fine hemp twine (1.2mm):
    2 pieces 44"/110cm long (c)
  Natural-color fine hemp twine (1.2mm):
    2 pieces 44"/110cm long (b)

Bottom sample:
  Moss Green fine hemp twine (1.2mm):
    2 pieces 40"/100cm long (a)
  Red fine hemp twine (1.2mm):
    2 pieces 44"/110cm long (b)
  Black fine hemp twine (1.2mm):
    2 pieces 44"/110cm long (c)

Middle sample:
  Golden fine hemp twine (1.2mm):
    2 pieces 40"/100cm long (a)
  Light Blue fine hemp twine (1.2mm):
    2 pieces 44"/110cm long (b)
  Natural-color fine hemp twine (1.2mm):
    2 pieces 44"/110cm long (c)

size

⅜" x 13½"/1cm x 34cm

tip

Two of our samples are made with 3 colors. The other has just 2 colors. Look at the photo to see how the effect differs, and at the Knotting Diagram (at right) to see how the colors move. Arrange your colors however you like.

① Starting off, in detail

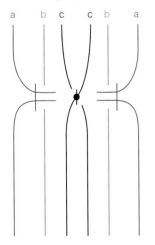

a b c   c b a

[instructions]

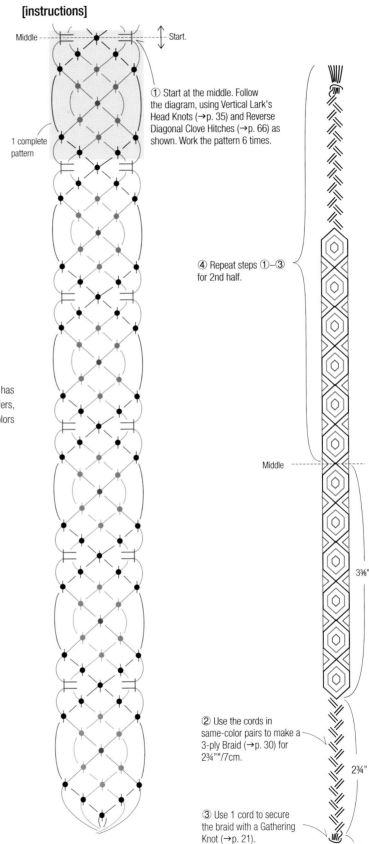

Middle ----   Start.

1 complete pattern

① Start at the middle. Follow the diagram, using Vertical Lark's Head Knots (→p. 35) and Reverse Diagonal Clove Hitches (→p. 66) as shown. Work the pattern 6 times.

④ Repeat steps ①–③ for 2nd half.

Middle ----

3⅜"

② Use the cords in same-color pairs to make a 3-ply Braid (→p. 30) for 2¾""/7cm.

2¾"

③ Use 1 cord to secure the braid with a Gathering Knot (→p. 21).

⅜"

18. braided handle   photo ... page 108

photo ... page 108

pattern: (20)

materials (for 2)

Tan leather flat cord (5mm):
    6 pieces 40"/100cm long
White medium hemp twine (1.8mm):
    4 pieces 40"/100cm long

size

12"/30cm long (including attachment loops)

tip

The dimensions specified are based on a space of ⅝"/1.5cm between the grommet and the top edge of the bag. Your bag may be different or you may prefer another handle length; allow more leather cord to suit your situation.

④ Attaching the finished handle, in detail

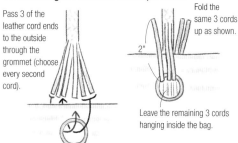

Pass 3 of the leather cord ends to the outside through the grommet (choose every second cord).

Fold the same 3 cords up as shown.

2"

Leave the remaining 3 cords hanging inside the bag.

[instructions]

③ Make a Round 6-ply Braid (→p. 46) 8¼"/21cm long.

8¼"

④ Refer to the detail at left to loop the cords through the grommet. Repeat step 2 to bind them. When you are finished, cut the extending ends of the leather cord flush above and below all the bindings.

¾"

② Using 1 piece of hemp twine, secure the cords above the bag with a Wrapping Knot (→p. 22).

Top edge of bag

Start.

Grommets

① Pass 3 of the leather cords through the grommet, folding in half to extend above it.

19. medallion handle   photo ... page 108

photo ... page 108

pattern: (05)(22)

materials (for 2)

Tan medium hemp twine (1.8mm):
    4 pieces 160"/400cm long; 4 pieces 40"/100cm long
Moss Green medium hemp twine (1.8mm):
    4 pieces 40"/100cm long
Sewing thread to match

size

27½"/70cm long (including 2"/5cm fringe)

tip

To lengthen or shorten the handles, adjust the length between the 2 Awaji Knots.

[instructions]

⑦ Trim the fringe ends evenly.

2"

Start.

⑤ Make 5 Left-facing Square Knots.

⑥ At each end, use 1 cord to secure the braid with a Gathering Knot (→p. 21).

④ Make a 3-cord Awaji Knot.

② Make a 3-cord Awaji Knot (→p. 47).

① Align the ends of the cords. Beginning 2¾"/7cm from the end, make 5 Left-facing Square Knots (→p. 31).

③ Make Left-facing Square Knots for 20"/50cm.

20"

Attaching the finished handle, in detail

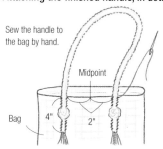

Sew the handle to the bag by hand.

Midpoint

Bag

4"   2"

① Cord sequence, in detail

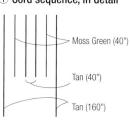

Moss Green (40")

Tan (40")

Tan (160")

20. zigzag strap   photo ... page 109

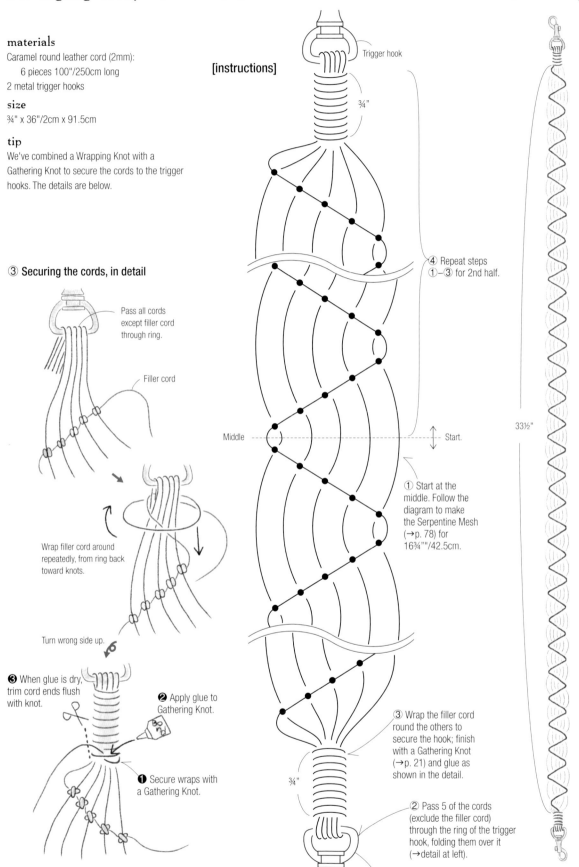

materials

Caramel round leather cord (2mm):
   6 pieces 100"/250cm long
2 metal trigger hooks

size

¾" x 36"/2cm x 91.5cm

tip

We've combined a Wrapping Knot with a Gathering Knot to secure the cords to the trigger hooks. The details are below.

③ Securing the cords, in detail

Pass all cords except filler cord through ring.

Filler cord

Wrap filler cord around repeatedly, from ring back toward knots.

Turn wrong side up.

❸ When glue is dry, trim cord ends flush with knot.

❷ Apply glue to Gathering Knot.

❶ Secure wraps with a Gathering Knot.

[instructions]

Trigger hook

¾"

④ Repeat steps ①–③ for 2nd half.

Middle

Start.

① Start at the middle. Follow the diagram to make the Serpentine Mesh (→p. 78) for 16¾"/42.5cm.

③ Wrap the filler cord round the others to secure the hook; finish with a Gathering Knot (→p. 21) and glue as shown in the detail.

② Pass 5 of the cords (exclude the filler cord) through the ring of the trigger hook, folding them over it (→detail at left).

¾"

Trigger hook

33½"

Chapter 03   Projects

137

17. watchbands   photo ... page 110

A   pattern: ⑲ ㊿

materials
Natural-color very fine leather cord (1mm): 8 pieces 40"/100cm long
1 wristwatch
1 decorative button for clasp

size
⅝" x 7½"/1.5cm x 19cm (not including the fringe)

tip
Make sure to adjust the length of the strap to fit the size of the watch and the wrist of the wearer.

B   pattern: ⑲ ㊾

materials
Off-white extra-fine cotton cord (0.8mm): 8 pieces 32"/80cm long
1 wristwatch
1 brass shank button for clasp

size
⅜" x 7½"/1cm x 19cm (not including the fringe)

tip
While you are knotting, test the loop size to make sure it will pass over the button.

[instructions]

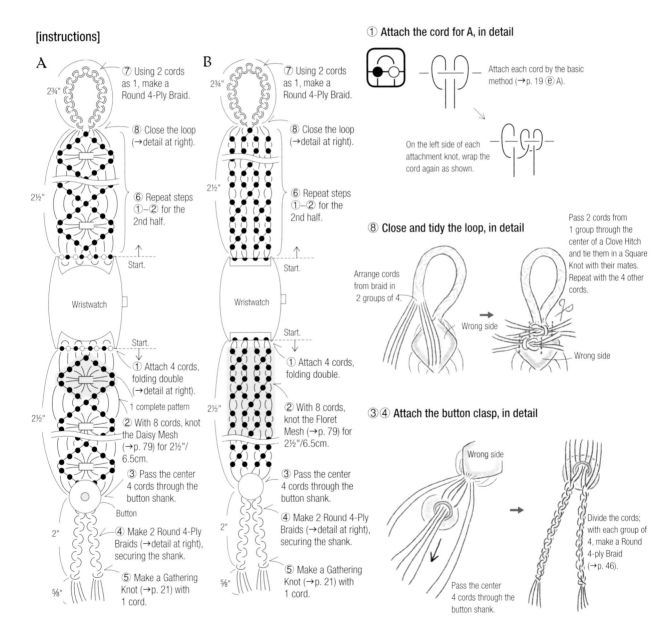

A
2¾"
⑦ Using 2 cords as 1, make a Round 4-Ply Braid.
⑧ Close the loop (→detail at right).
2½"
⑥ Repeat steps ①–② for the 2nd half.
2½"
Start.
Wristwatch
Start.
① Attach 4 cords, folding double (→detail at right).
1 complete pattern
② With 8 cords, knot the Daisy Mesh (→p. 79) for 2½"/6.5cm.
2½"
③ Pass the center 4 cords through the button shank.
Button
2"
④ Make 2 Round 4-Ply Braids (→detail at right), securing the shank.
⑤ Make a Gathering Knot (→p. 21) with 1 cord.
⅝"

B
2¾"
⑦ Using 2 cords as 1, make a Round 4-Ply Braid.
⑧ Close the loop (→detail at right).
2½"
⑥ Repeat steps ①–② for the 2nd half.
Start.
Wristwatch
Start.
① Attach 4 cords, folding double.
② With 8 cords, knot the Floret Mesh (→p. 79) for 2½"/6.5cm.
2½"
③ Pass the center 4 cords through the button shank.
④ Make 2 Round 4-Ply Braids (→detail at right), securing the shank.
2"
⑤ Make a Gathering Knot (→p. 21) with 1 cord.
⅝"

① Attach the cord for A, in detail

Attach each cord by the basic method (→p. 19 ⓔ A).

On the left side of each attachment knot, wrap the cord again as shown.

⑧ Close and tidy the loop, in detail

Arrange cords from braid in 2 groups of 4.

Wrong side

Pass 2 cords from 1 group through the center of a Clove Hitch and tie them in a Square Knot with their mates. Repeat with the 4 other cords.

Wrong side

③④ Attach the button clasp, in detail

Wrong side

Pass the center 4 cords through the button shank.

Divide the cords; with each group of 4, make a Round 4-ply Braid (→p. 46).

22. camera strap   photo ... page III

materials

Natural-color fine hemp rope (2mm):
    4 pieces 140"/350cm long (a)
Olive fine hemp rope (2mm):
    4 pieces 152"/380cm long (b)
2 split rings (20mm)

size

1" x 32¾"/2.5cm x 83cm

tip

This variation of the Wood Grain Mesh can be made any length you like. Make sure it is the length you want before finishing off the ends.

②③ Finish the ends, in detail

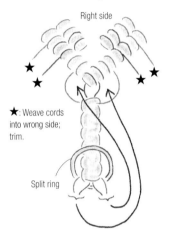

Right side

★: Weave cords into wrong side; trim.

Split ring

Make a sennit with 6 Square Knots (→p. 31; center 2 cords are filler cords). Pass through the split ring, folding in half to make a loop.

↓

Turn over; at each edge, pass 2 cords through the top of the sennit and then tie together across the sennit in a Square Knot to secure the loop. Apply glue to the knot; weave in and trim the ends.

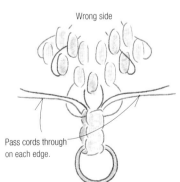

Wrong side

Pass cords through on each edge.

[instructions]

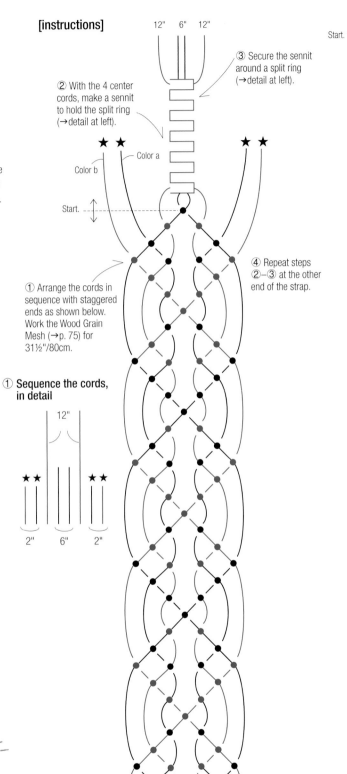

12"   6"   12"

③ Secure the sennit around a split ring (→detail at left).

② With the 4 center cords, make a sennit to hold the split ring (→detail at left).

★ ★   ★ ★

Color a

Color b

Start.

① Arrange the cords in sequence with staggered ends as shown below. Work the Wood Grain Mesh (→p. 75) for 31½"/80cm.

④ Repeat steps ②–③ at the other end of the strap.

① Sequence the cords, in detail

12"

★ ★   ★ ★

2"   6"   2"

Start.

⅝"

31½"

Chapter 03   Projects

139

materials

Off-white extra-fine cotton cord (0.8mm):
- 1 piece 280"/700cm long (working cord)
- 1 piece 40"/100cm long (filler cord)

17 small pearl beads (5–6mm)

Sewing thread to match

size

1¼" x 13"/3cm x 33cm

tip

This is a variation of the Vertical Lark's Head Lace Band on p. 93 – narrower, more delicate, and with pearl beads added to the Picots on 1 edge. Make it any length you like, to trim something gorgeous. Follow the diagrams to make the knots face right or left (→p. 35).

① Cord arrangement, in detail

Working cord
Filler cord
20" 20"
136" 136"

How to attach the braid

Lap the braid over the edge of your item; sew in place by hand with tiny stitches.

[instructions]

Start.

① Align the midpoints of the cords; make 1 Right-facing Vertical Lark's Head Knot (→detail at left).

¼" ¼" ½"

Pearl bead

② Follow the diagram to make Picots between the 3rd and 4th, 5th and 6th, and 7th and 8th Lark's Head Knots. For the middle Picot, thread a pearl bead onto the cord.

③ Follow the diagram, making the Picots all the same length on this side.

④ Twist the 2 filler cords around each other.

⑤ Final motif, in detail

Left working cord Right working cord
Left filler cord Right filler cord

⑤ Repeat steps ②–④ until the trim is the desired length (17 motifs = 13"/33cm). After final repeat, do not twist the filler cords (→detail at left).

⑨ Pass the left working cord from front to back through the knot marked △ (red).

⑩ Cut the ends of the 4 cords short.

⑥ Pass both cords on the right from front to back through the knot on the left ♡ (red).

⑦ Pass both cords on the left from front to back through the knot on the right △ (red).

⑧ Make a Left-facing Vertical Lark's Head Knot with the left working cord.

Start.
13"

Pearl bead

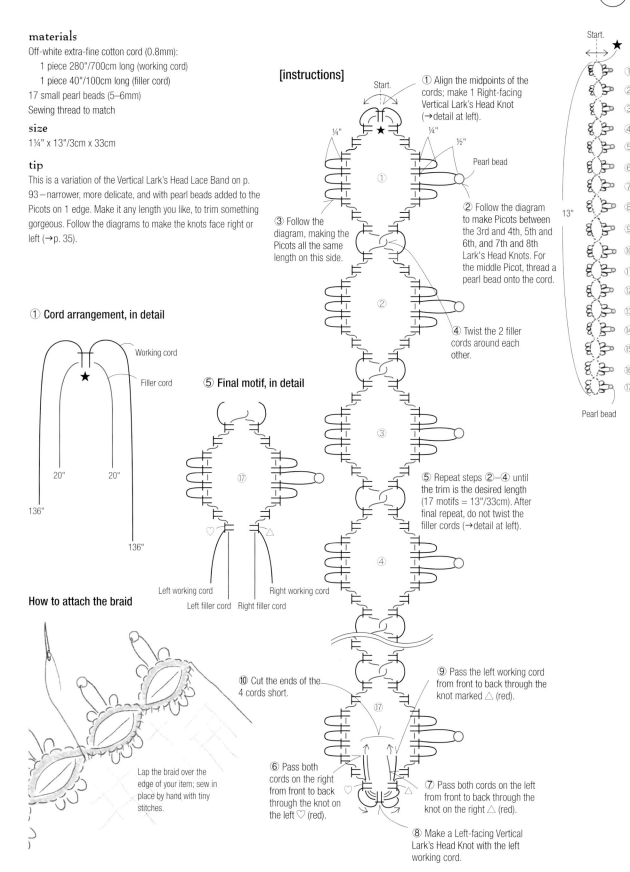

24. fringed diamond border   photo ... page 113   pattern: (41) (60) (64)

materials (for 13½"/34cm width)

Red fine hemp twine (1.2mm):

   72 pieces 40"/100cm long (vertical cords)

   3 pieces 24"/60cm long (anchor cords)

Sewing thread to match

size

13½" x 7½" deep/34cm x 19cm deep (depth includes 3⅛"/8cm fringe)

tip

The horizontal repeat of this pattern (1 diamond, 12 vertical cords folded double) is 2¼"/5.5cm. Divide the width of the item you wish to decorate by 2¼"/5.5cm; round up or down to the nearest whole number then multiply by 12 to see how many vertical cords you need. If you rounded up or down, space the cords looser or tighter to compensate. These instructions are for 6 repeats.

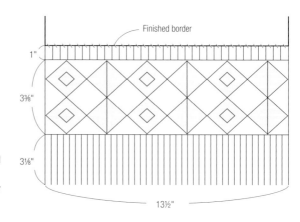

[instructions]

① Fold each vertical cord in half; attach to 1 anchor cord. Make Square Knot sennits (→p. 31) across as shown.

② Tie the vertical cords in Horizontal Clove Hitches to another anchor cord.

③ Follow the diagram to work the 2 diamond patterns (→p. 91 and p. 90), alternating them across for a total of 6 motifs, or as needed for your size. Make this section 2 diamonds deep as shown.

⑥ Neatly weave in all anchor cord ends; trim excess.

④ Repeat step 2.

⑤ Cut neatly (→detail above).

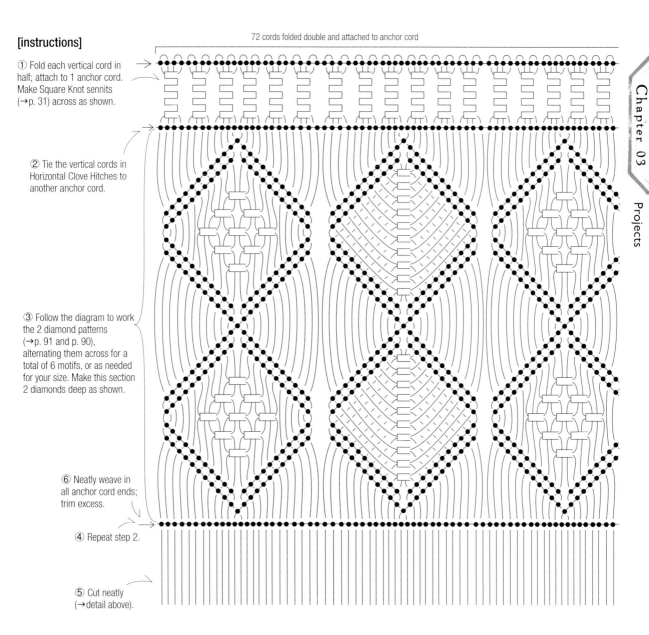

72 cords folded double and attached to anchor cord

materials

Black Snowflake:
Natural-color medium hemp twine (1.8mm):
18½ yards/16m30cm (color a)
Black medium hemp twine (1.8mm):
cut into lengths shown next to diagram below (color b)

White Snowflake:
Black medium hemp twine (1.8mm):
18½ yards/16m30cm (color a)
Natural-color medium hemp twine (1.8mm):
cut into lengths shown next to diagram below (color b)

size

4½" x 5"/11.5cm x 12.5cm (h x w)

tip

This coaster is made from the Cavandoli Snowflake Tapestry
pattern on p. 98, just as is, but in order make the edges as
similar as possible, we started by attaching single vertical
cords with the fringe method. Then when finished, we tucked
the extending ends at the top and bottom into the knots on the
wrong side of the work.

Black snowflake

4½"

5"

White snowflake

[instructions]

Color b

A E A B B B D B B C B C B B C C C C B B C B C B B D B B B A E A

Color a →

① Attach the 33 color b cords
to the anchor cord using the
Fringe Method (→ ⓕ p. 20).

Lengths for vertical cords
A = 12"/30cm
B = 24"/60cm
C = 28"/70cm
D = 32"/80cm
E = 40"/100cm

② Follow the chart and the
knot key below to work the
snowflake pattern.

③ Weave all the cord ends into
the knots on wrong side; cut off
the excess.

□ Vertical Clove Hitch

▨ Horizontal Clove Hitch

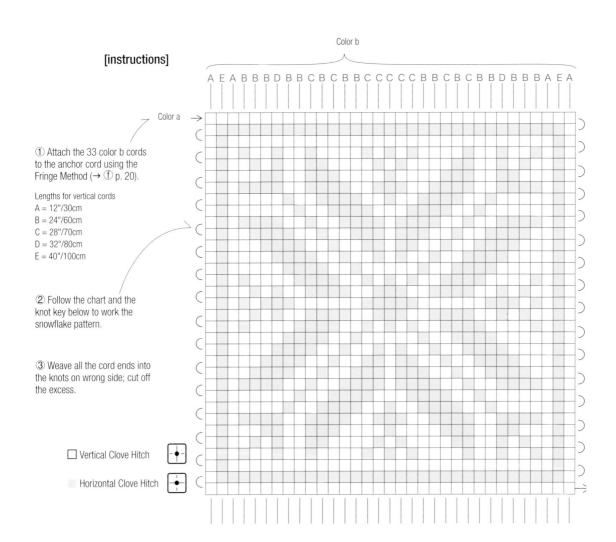

26. striped hot pad   photo ... page 114

materials

Fine hemp rope (2mm):

    Natural-color: 13 pieces 52"/130cm long

    Bright Red: 12 pieces 52"/130cm long; 1 piece 60"/150cm long (anchor cord)

size

5⅛" x 5 ⅜"/13cm x 13.5cm (h x w)

tip

This interpretation of the Twisted Buddhist Treasure Mesh (→p. 63) is set up with pairs of working cords in 2 alternating colors, which create a stripe as the Spiral Knot sennits are offset every few rows. You can easily change the size by using more working cords or knotting more rows of the pattern.

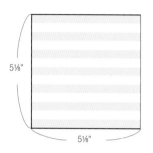

③ **Bring the cord ends to the back, in detail**

Wrap each working cord from back to front under and then over the anchor cord; insert to back.

Anchor cord

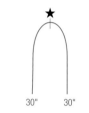

★

30"   30"

[instructions]

① Fold the anchor cord in half. Attach the working cords to the right half: Begin at the middle with Natural and then alternate the colors.

Bright Red
Natural

★   60"

② Follow the diagram to work 13 stripes (each circled numeral = 1 stripe).

③ Wrap the end of each working cord over the anchor cord; insert to the back. Tie each pair in a Square Knot. Weave in the ends.

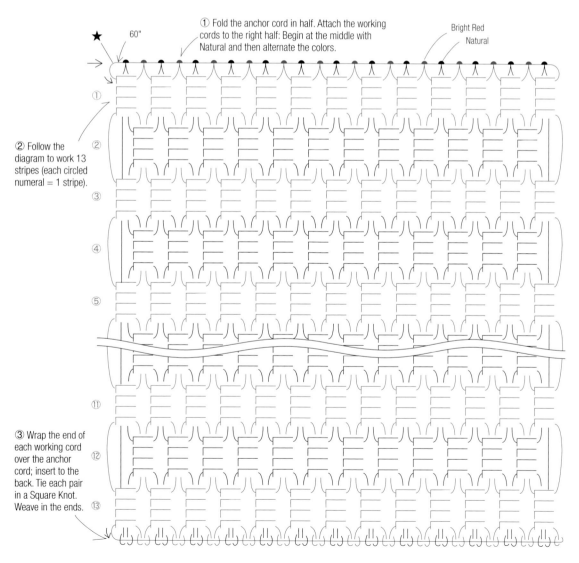

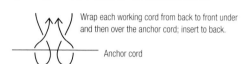

materials

Soft jute cord (2mm; colors listed from center out):

Yellow Ochre: 27 yards/9m20cm

Terra-cotta: 13 yards/11m50cm

Red: 24 yards/21m10cm

White: 76 yards/67m70cm

Refer to the table at right to cut the cords.

size

12"/30cm in diameter

tip

The Circular Flower on p. 95 has grown from posy to giant bloom! This mat is made in the same way the smaller one is, but with many more rows of "petals" (→p. 95 for complete knotting directions).

[Cord Cutting Guide]

	Color	Filler cord (1 each)	Working cords (2 each)
Center	Yellow Ochre	12"/30cm	-
Round ①	Yellow Ochre	20"/50cm	24"/60cm
Round ②	Yellow Ochre	32"/80cm	44"/110cm
Round ③	Yellow Ochre	40"/100cm	64"/160cm
Round ④	Terra-cotta	48"/120cm	80"/200cm
Round ⑤	Terra-cotta	52"/130cm	100"/250cm
Round ⑥	Red	64"/160cm	112"/280cm
Round ⑦	White	72"/180cm	132"/330cm
Round ⑧	White	80"/200cm	152"/380cm
Round ⑨	White	84"/210cm	168"/420cm
Round ⑩	White	92"/230cm	192"/480cm
Round ⑪	White	100"/250cm	200"/500cm
Round ⑫	Red	108"/270cm	224"/560cm
Round ⑬	White	112"/280cm	240"/600cm

① Make a round of petals, in detail

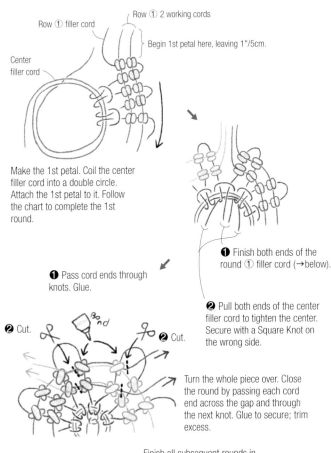

Row ① filler cord

Row ① 2 working cords

Begin 1st petal here, leaving 1"/5cm.

Center filler cord

Make the 1st petal. Coil the center filler cord into a double circle. Attach the 1st petal to it. Follow the chart to complete the 1st round.

❶ Pass cord ends through knots. Glue.

❷ Cut.   Bond   ❷ Cut.

❶ Finish both ends of the round ① filler cord (→below).

❷ Pull both ends of the center filler cord to tighten the center. Secure with a Square Knot on the wrong side.

Turn the whole piece over. Close the round by passing each cord end across the gap and through the next knot. Glue to secure; trim excess.

Finish all subsequent rounds in the same way.

Connect the petals, in detail

To keep the mat from separating into loose skinny strips as its circumference grows larger, you need to attach each new round to the previous one more frequently than in the beginning. The stars on the knotting diagram show where to make these connections. The drawing below shows how to loop the active filler cord through the "petal" of the previous round.

previous round   new round

[instructions]

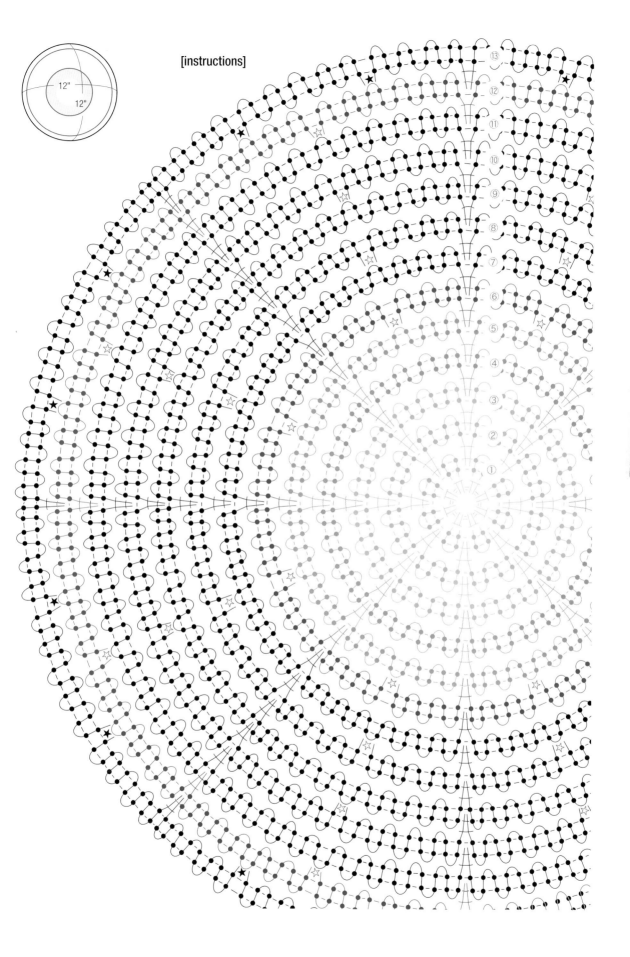

28. net bag   photo ... page 116

materials
Yellow Ochre soft jute cord (2mm):
 16 pieces 80"/200cm long (for bag)
 2 pieces 120"/300cm long (to wrap handles)

size
Approximately 11"/28cm deep (→photo)

tip
The bag is worked from the bottom up, as a tube. The handles are easy
to make: Each is just a bundle of knotting cords from the bag, completely
wrapped together with another cord. The key to a good-looking handle is
to wrap it neatly and tightly without any gaps.

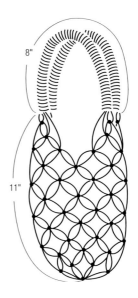

8"

11"

④ **Make the handles, in detail**

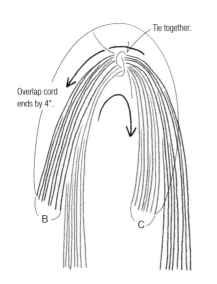

Tie together.

Overlap cord
ends by 4".

B   C

Overlap cord groups B and C by 4"/10cm. Secure
in the middle by tying with a scrap of cord. Repeat
to overlap groups A and D.

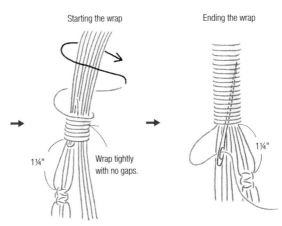

Starting the wrap

Ending the wrap

1¼"   Wrap tightly
            with no gaps.

1¼"

Using one 120"/300cm cord, begin wrapping at 1 end of the
handle, about 1¼"/3cm above the highest knots of the bag.
Stop 1¼"/3cm above the knots at the other end. Insert the end
of the wrapping cord up and under the wraps; bring it out and
cut off the excess.

[instructions]

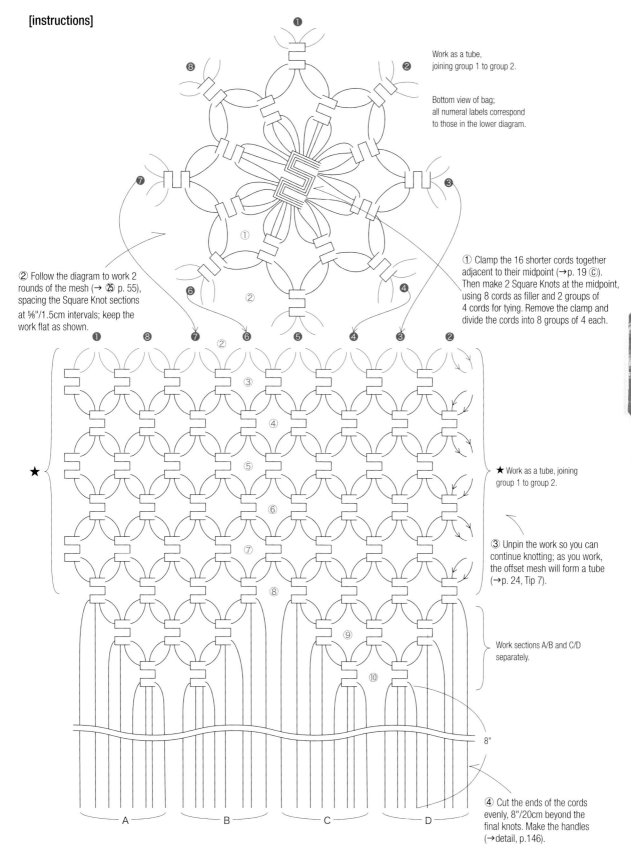

Work as a tube,
joining group 1 to group 2.

Bottom view of bag;
all numeral labels correspond
to those in the lower diagram.

② Follow the diagram to work 2
rounds of the mesh (→ ㉕ p. 55),
spacing the Square Knot sections
at ⅝"/1.5cm intervals; keep the
work flat as shown.

① Clamp the 16 shorter cords together
adjacent to their midpoint (→p. 19 Ⓒ).
Then make 2 Square Knots at the midpoint,
using 8 cords as filler and 2 groups of
4 cords for tying. Remove the clamp and
divide the cords into 8 groups of 4 each.

★ Work as a tube, joining
group 1 to group 2.

③ Unpin the work so you can
continue knotting; as you work,
the offset mesh will form a tube
(→p. 24, Tip 7).

Work sections A/B and C/D
separately.

8"

④ Cut the ends of the cords
evenly, 8"/20cm beyond the
final knots. Make the handles
(→detail, p.146).

materials

Blue medium hemp twine (1.8cm):
  2 pieces 92"/230cm long (for the top rim)
  40 pieces 40"/100cm long (for the working cords)
  4 pieces 52"/130cm long (for the handles)

size

8" x 8"/20cm x 20cm; handles are 8"/20cm long

tip

A long Square Knot sennit is shaped into a ring for the top of this bag; then the cords for the mesh are tied onto it and knotted. Before the handles are knotted, 1 end of their cords is attached to the rim; the other end is attached when the handles have been knotted to the right length.

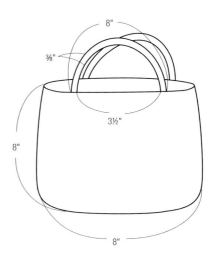

① **Make the top rim, in detail**

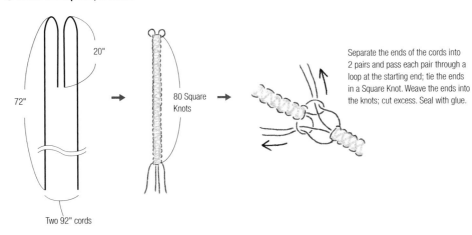

Separate the ends of the cords into 2 pairs and pass each pair through a loop at the starting end; tie the ends in a Square Knot. Weave the ends into the knots; cut excess. Seal with glue.

⑤ **Square Knot with extra twist, in detail**

⑥ **Attach the handle, in detail**

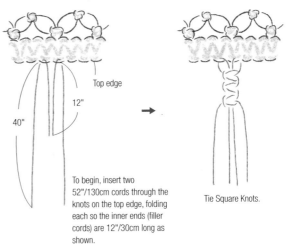

To begin, insert two 52"/130cm cords through the knots on the top edge, folding each so the inner ends (filler cords) are 12"/30cm long as shown.

Tie Square Knots.

[instructions]

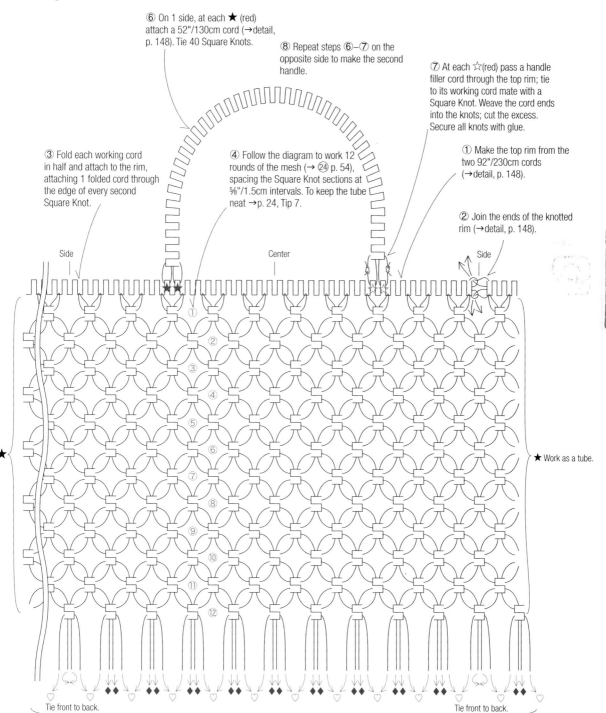

⑥ On 1 side, at each ★ (red) attach a 52"/130cm cord (→detail, p. 148). Tie 40 Square Knots.

⑧ Repeat steps ⑥–⑦ on the opposite side to make the second handle.

⑦ At each ☆(red) pass a handle filler cord through the top rim; tie to its working cord mate with a Square Knot. Weave the cord ends into the knots; cut the excess. Secure all knots with glue.

③ Fold each working cord in half and attach to the rim, attaching 1 folded cord through the edge of every second Square Knot.

④ Follow the diagram to work 12 rounds of the mesh (→ ㉔ p. 54), spacing the Square Knot sections at ⅝"/1.5cm intervals. To keep the tube neat →p. 24, Tip 7.

① Make the top rim from the two 92"/230cm cords (→detail, p. 148).

② Join the ends of the knotted rim (→detail, p. 148).

Side

Center

Side

★

★ Work as a tube.

Tie front to back.

Tie front to back.

⑤ Turn the bag inside out; flatten the tube, aligning the mesh. At each ◆ (red), tie the front cord to the back cord (→⑤ detail, p. 148). At each ♡ (red) tie the neighboring cords in a Square Knot. Secure all knots with glue; cut the excess cord.

30. diamond tote bag   photo ... page 118

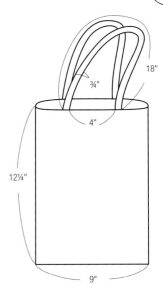

materials
Natural-color medium hemp twine (1.8cm)
- 84 pieces 108"/270cm long (for the vertical cords)
- 2 pieces 32"/80cm long (for the anchor cords)
- 8 pieces 60"/150cm long (for the handles)
- 8 pieces 44"/110cm long (for the handles)

Red medium hemp twine (1.8cm)
- 14 pieces 60"/150cm (for the accent vertical cords)

size
9" x 12¼"/23cm x 31 cm (w x h); handles are 18"/45cm long

tip
The bag and handles are worked separately and joined when finished. Each handle is a narrow strip of Buddhist Treasure Mesh A, knotted without gaps, with about 3"/7cm unknotted cords at each end used to tie it to the bag. To knot the tube without tangles (→p. 24, Tip 7).

① Set up the tote rim, in detail

Fold the natural-color cords double; attach with alternating extra wraps.

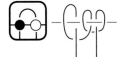 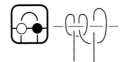

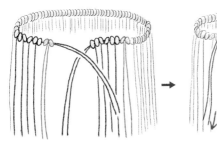

Hold the anchor cords together as 1 and begin about 4"/10cm from 1 end. Refer to the diagram on p.151 to attach the vertical cords in a repeating sequence of 1 doubled red cord and 6 doubled natural cords. Attach all but 4 of the cords.

Overlap the ends of the anchor cords. Attach the remaining vertical cords over the overlapped anchor cords. Then use a large-eyed needle to pass the anchor cords through a few knots in each direction; bring out and cut off the excess.

④ Attach the handles, in detail

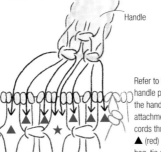

Handle

Top of bag, outside

Refer to the diagram on page 151 to locate the handle positions. With the outside ofboth the bag and the handle facing you, align the handle end above the attachment position as shown at left. Pass the handle cords through the bag, inserting 1 at each ▲ (red) and 2 at the ★ (red). On the inside of the bag, tie each pair of handle cords in a Square Knot (→p. 21). Repeat at each attachment position.

Handle Knotting Diagram →p. 54

Handle cord sequence

44"   60"   44"

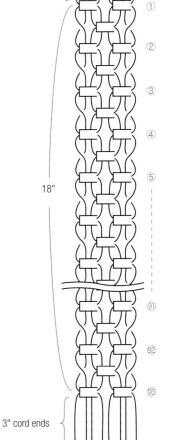

3" cord ends

① ② ③ ④ ⑤

18"

91 92 93

3" cord ends

[bag instructions]

Start.

Red accent cord

Natural cords

Center

① Attach the vertical working cords to the anchor cords (→detail, p. 150).

④ Attach handles here (→detail, p. 150).

Side

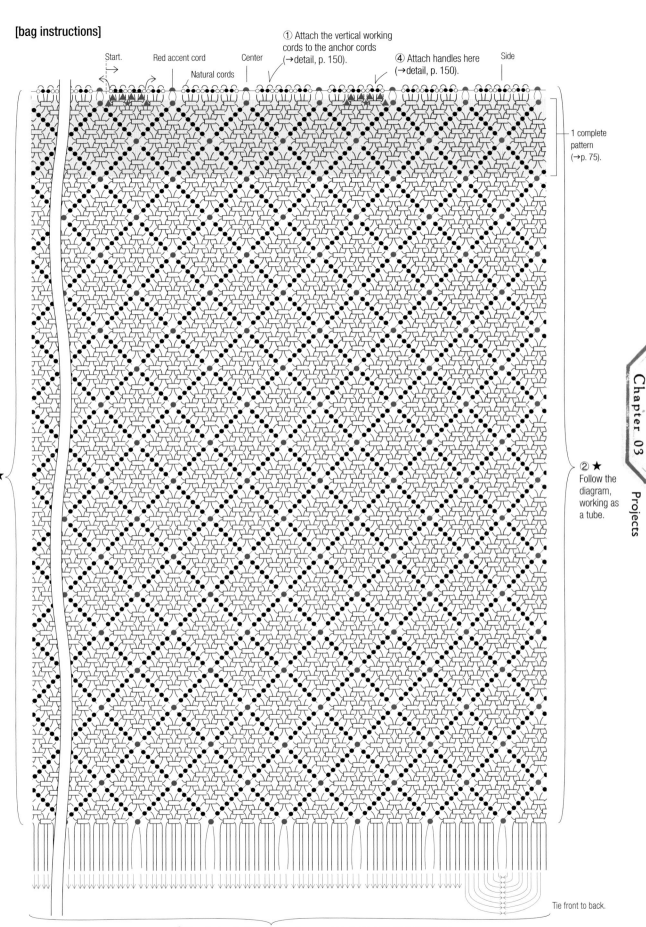

1 complete pattern (→p. 75).

★

② ★
Follow the diagram, working as a tube.

Tie front to back.

③ Turn the bag inside out; align the accent cords. Tie each front cord to the corresponding back cord, using 2 Square Knots with an extra twist (→148). Secure all knots with glue; cut the excess cord.

31. small striped bag   photo ... page 119

materials

White medium hemp twine (1.8cm)

    40 pieces 80"/200cm long (for the vertical cords)

    1 piece 20"/50cm long (the for anchor cords)

    4 pieces 80"/200cm (for the handles); 4 pieces 112"/280cm long

    (for the handles)

Natural-color medium hemp twine (1.8cm)

    40 pieces 80"/200cm long (for the vertical cords)

size

6¾" x 10⅝"/17 cm x 27cm(w x h); handles are 18"/46cm long

tip

Each handle is a narrow strip of Buddhist Treasure Mesh A, knotted without gaps. Make the bag first, then attach the handle cords to the top rim and knot the strips — you'll attach their other end when finished.

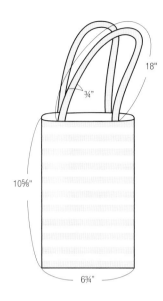

① Make the handles, in detail

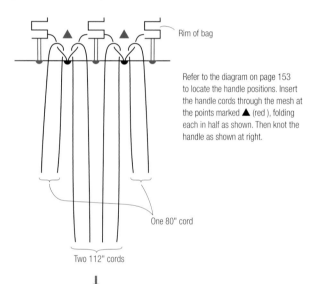

Rim of bag

Refer to the diagram on page 153 to locate the handle positions. Insert the handle cords through the mesh at the points marked ▲ (red), folding each in half as shown. Then knot the handle as shown at right.

One 80" cord

Two 112" cords

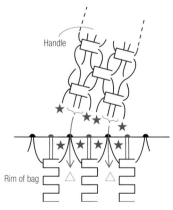

Handle

When the handle knotting is finished, insert the cord ends to the inside through the mesh marked ★ (red) on the diagram on p. 153; then tie each pair in a Square Knot where marked by a △ (red). Pass the ends through knots on the inside; trim the excess.

Rim of bag

Handle Knotting Diagram → p. 54

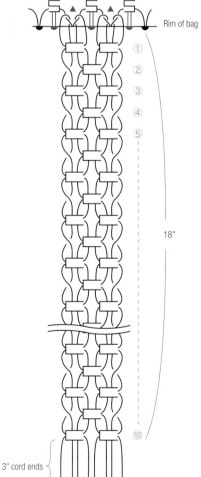

Rim of bag

① ② ③ ④ ⑤

18"

93

3" cord ends

[bag instructions]

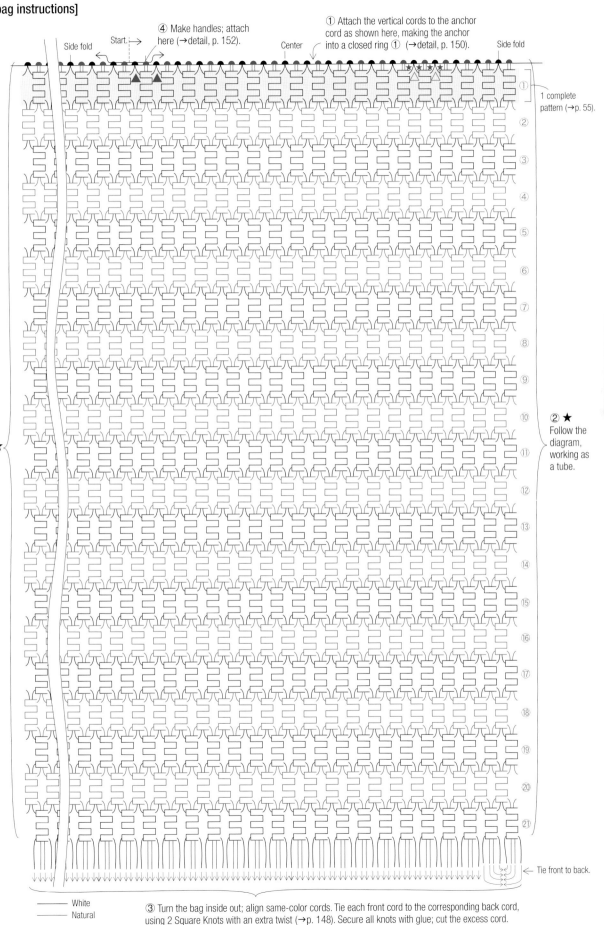

④ Make handles; attach here (→detail, p. 152).

① Attach the vertical cords to the anchor cord as shown here, making the anchor into a closed ring ① (→detail, p. 150).

Side fold   Start.   Center   Side fold

1 complete pattern (→p. 55).

② ★
Follow the diagram, working as a tube.

—— White
—— Natural

← Tie front to back.

③ Turn the bag inside out; align same-color cords. Tie each front cord to the corresponding back cord, using 2 Square Knots with an extra twist (→p. 148). Secure all knots with glue; cut the excess cord.

32. harvest basket   photo ... page 120   pattern: (05) (23) (35) (54)

materials

Natural-color sisal (3mm), raffia, or sea grass rope*
    84 pieces 64"/160cm long (basket body vertical cords)
    6 pieces 40"/100cm long (basket body anchor cords)
    1 piece 200"/500cm long (handle working cords)
    2 pieces 40"/100cm long (handle filler cords)
Red soft 3-ply jute cord: 14 pieces 20"/50cm long

size

3¾" x 12" x 4¾"/9cm x 30cm x 12cm (w x l x h);
handle is 13"/33cm long

*About the cord: The sample in the photo is made from 3mm Lupis rope
(abaca fiber), a quality of sisal twine not widely available in the U.S.
Conventional sisal, raffia, or seagrass may be substituted but the lengths
required and the knot size may be different: Make a swatch (→p. 24, Tip 4)
Dampen these cords to make them supple for knotting.

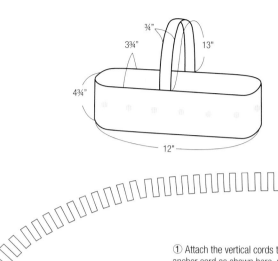

[instructions]

⑥ Follow the dashed lines in the pink area to insert the cord ends to the back; tie in Square Knots in pairs; secure with glue and cut excess.

① Attach the vertical cords to the anchor cord as shown here, making the anchor into a closed ring (→① detail, p. 150).

Start. →

64" vertical cords

Midpoint of 1 end

40" anchor →
40" anchor →
40" anchor →

★

40" anchor →

40" anchor →
40" anchor →

4   4   4   4   4

Tie edges together.

③ Turn the bag inside out, folding at the ends to create a flat oval bottom. Tie corresponding cords together, using 2 Square Knots with an extra twist (→p. 148). Secure all knots with glue; cut the excess cord.

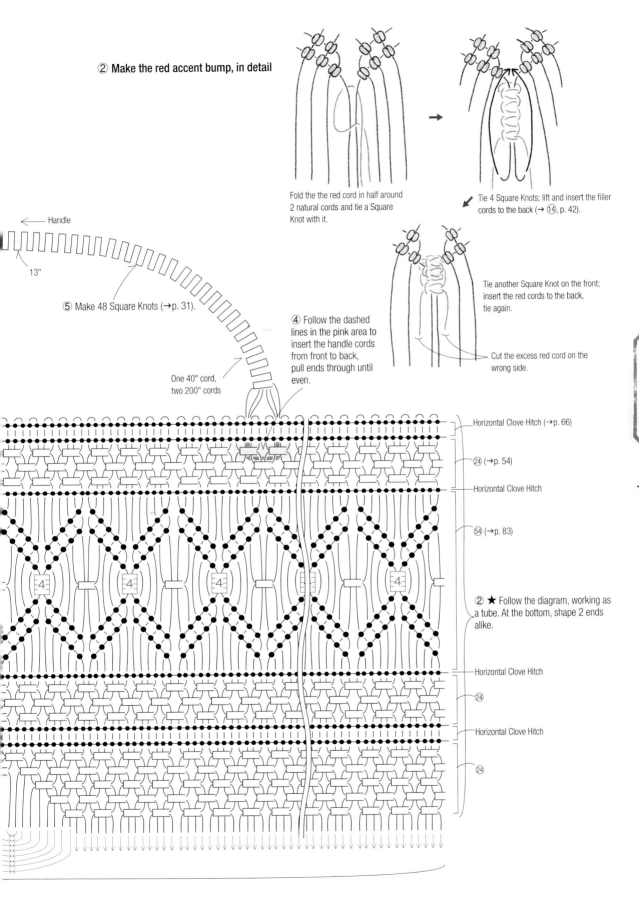

② Make the red accent bump, in detail

Fold the the red cord in half around 2 natural cords and tie a Square Knot with it.

↙ Tie 4 Square Knots; lift and insert the filler cords to the back (→ ⑭, p. 42).

Tie another Square Knot on the front; insert the red cords to the back, tie again.

—— Cut the excess red cord on the wrong side.

← Handle

13"

⑤ Make 48 Square Knots (→p. 31).

One 40" cord, two 200" cords

④ Follow the dashed lines in the pink area to insert the handle cords from front to back, pull ends through until even.

Horizontal Clove Hitch (→p. 66)

㉔ (→ p. 54)

Horizontal Clove Hitch

㊴ (→p. 83)

② ★ Follow the diagram, working as a tube. At the bottom, shape 2 ends alike.

Horizontal Clove Hitch

㉔

Horizontal Clove Hitch

㉔

33. retro handbag photo ... page 122

materials

Leaf Green soft jute cord (2mm)

    36 pieces 120"/300cm long (A on diagram)

    20 pieces 100"/250cm long (B on diagram)

1 rosewood ring handle (4½"/11cm interior width)

size

8" x 8"/20cm x 20cm; 4"/10cm wide at handle

tip

Because the mesh pattern of this bag creates a slightly scalloped edge, the bottom of the bag requires a special tying method to close the gaps: Instead of tying each cord on the front to the corresponding cord on the back, crisscross some of the cords to form an X across the bottom as you tie. The symbols on the diagram indicate which cords to cross.

② **Add cords to widen the work, in detail**

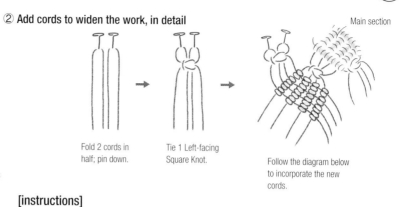

Fold 2 cords in half; pin down.

Tie 1 Left-facing Square Knot.

Main section

Follow the diagram below to incorporate the new cords.

[instructions]

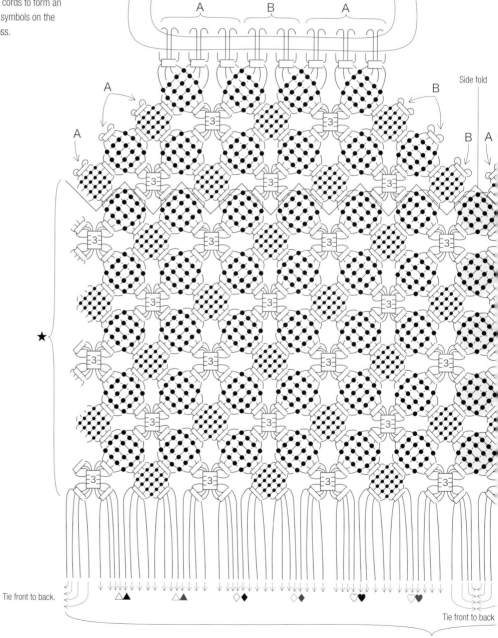

Tie front to back.

Tie front to back

④ Turn the bag inside out, softly folding at the sides (shaded pink). Using 2 Square Knots with an extra twist (→p. 148), tie the cords of each layer together; cross the symbol-marked cords between the layers to close the gaps. Secure all knots with glue; cut the excess cord.

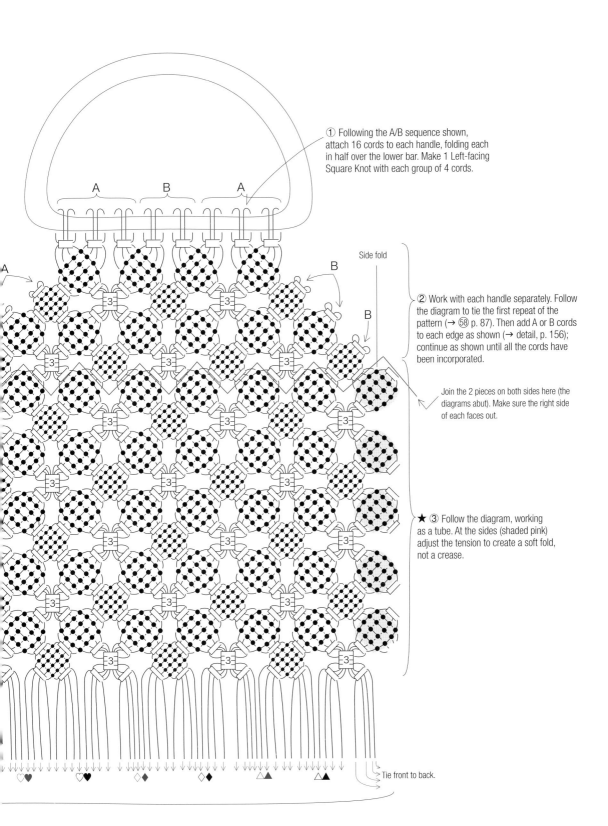

① Following the A/B sequence shown, attach 16 cords to each handle, folding each in half over the lower bar. Make 1 Left-facing Square Knot with each group of 4 cords.

Side fold

② Work with each handle separately. Follow the diagram to tie the first repeat of the pattern (→ ⑤⑧ p. 87). Then add A or B cords to each edge as shown (→ detail, p. 156); continue as shown until all the cords have been incorporated.

Join the 2 pieces on both sides here (the diagrams abut). Make sure the right side of each faces out.

★ ③ Follow the diagram, working as a tube. At the sides (shaded pink) adjust the tension to create a soft fold, not a crease.

Tie front to back.

About the author and supervisor

Märchen Art Studio

This is the creative group that supervises Märchen-Art Company in Japan, which designs and sells leather and hemp cords, accessory parts, and other craft items. As well as having a shop/workshop in the Ryogoku district of Tokyo, the group publishes works in books and magazines, creates fashionable items in distinctive materials, and proposes new ways to enjoy macramé. We regret their materials are not easily found in the U.S.

The Japan Macramé Association

Founded in 1978 to advance and spread the craft of macramé. Since then, the group has organized regular training courses, research meetings, artwork competitions, and regional exhibitions, and is continuing activities promoting the techniques and charm of macramé. The group is also active in training instructors, issuing teaching certification, and publishing works on macramé.

Macramé Pattern Book

Märchen Art Studio

Supervised by The Japan Macramé Association

First designed and published in Japan in 2011 by
Graphic-sha Publishing Co., Ltd.
1-14-17 Kudankita, Chiyoda-ku, Tokyo 102-0073, Japan
Copyright © 2011 Marchen Art Studio
Copyright © 2011 Graphic-sha Publishing Co., Ltd.

English edition published in the United States of America in 2013 by
St. Martin's Press
175 Fifth Avenue, New York, N.Y. 10010
www.stmartins.com

Translation copyright © 2013 by St. Martin's Press

ISBN 978-1-250-03401-4
First U.S. Edition: May 2013
10 9

Creative staff
Author: Märchen Art Studio
Supervisor: The Japan Macramé Association
Planning and editing: Yoshiko Kasai (Graphic-sha Publishing Co., Ltd.)
Sample design and production: The Japan Macramé Association, design room
Illustrations: Yuriho Koike
Photographs: Ayako Hachisu
Book design: Kazaito seisakushitsu

English edition
English translation: Meher McArthur
Translation editing: Carol Spier
English edition layout: Shinichi Ishioka

Translation and editing of this edition coordinated by LibriSource Inc.

Production and management: Kumiko Sakamoto (Graphic-sha Publishing Co., Ltd.)

Printed and bound in China